Praise for *Water and Fire Survival Handbook*

"MacWelch is able to take very serious, sometimes even dire, survival scenarios and write about them in an accessible way. His writing is easy to digest and most importantly, it makes you want to get out and practice the skills and concepts he covers. His latest book should be mandatory reading for all outdoor enthusiasts."

—**Alex Robinson**, editor-in-chief of *Outdoor Life* magazine

"Tim MacWelch clearly walks the walk and knows firsthand what's involved with staying alive in the backcountry in addition to being a talented teacher who brilliantly relays the essential know-how for surviving in the wilds. Anyone who ventures outdoors should soak up the field-tested information in this practical handbook!"

—**Tony Nester**, author and owner of
Ancient Pathways Survival School

"Survival is more than just guns, knives, and self-defense techniques. It's also knowing how to stave off waterborne pathogens and create fire. That's why this book is a must-read. Tim's writing is both incredibly engaging and packed full of life-saving wisdom."

—**Patrick Vuong**, owner of Tiga Tactics and
former head editor of *Recoil Offgrid* Magazine

WATER AND FIRE SURVIVAL HANDBOOK

YOUR GUIDE TO PROVIDING SAFE DRINKING WATER AND STARTING A CAMPFIRE WITH VARIOUS METHODS

Tim MacWelch

Skyhorse Publishing

Skyhorse Publishing books may be purchased in bulk at special discounts for sales promotion, corporate gifts, fundraising, or educational purposes. Special editions can also be created to specifications. For details, contact the Special Sales Department, Skyhorse Publishing, 307 Fifth Avenue, 4th Floor, New York, NY 10016 or info@skyhorsepublishing.com.

Skyhorse® and Skyhorse Publishing® are registered trademarks of Skyhorse Publishing, Inc.®, a Delaware corporation.

Visit our website at www.skyhorsepublishing.com.

10 9 8 7 6 5 4 3 2 1

Library of Congress Control Number: 2026935773

Cover design by Kai Texel
Cover photos by Getty Images
All other images courtesy of the author

Print ISBN: 978-1-5107-8843-5
Ebook ISBN: 978-1-5107-8844-2

Printed in China

To my students—For the past thirty years you have repaid my survival lessons with two excellent gifts: your time and your friendship. My "repeat offender" students are my favorites, supporting me by taking many classes and encouraging me to continue my work, year after year. Thank you, Jae and Kayla, Brenna and Amelie, Michael B., Steve M., Jess, Carl C., Roman, Natalie, and so many others.

I'd like to especially thank my wife, Jenn, for supporting my teaching and writing careers for all these years. And finally, I dedicate this book to my daughters, Megan and Kaitlyn, who have spent their entire lives supporting their dad's unconventional choice to be a survival instructor.

Contents

Introduction

It may seem a little strange to pick up a survival book that focuses on both water and fire, but there is method to our madness. While these two elements may appear to be mortal enemies—the one extinguishing fire, the other evaporating water—you'll need water *and* you'll need the ability to ignite and control fire if you want to last for more than a few days in the wild. With a fire burning brightly in your survival camp, you can boil your water to make it safe for drinking. With some water standing nearby, you can put out that fire safely and effectively, eliminating the chance of starting a wildfire. Water and fire are inextricably linked to each other—two powerful allies in the fight for life. We should never forget that without water we could never have fire since we need water to grow the vegetation that becomes our fuel. So, don't think of water and fire as enemies or opposites of each other. Together they have the potential to be our friends in the wild places, but we need to know how to acquire them both, and with a little training and dedication to the crafts, how to put them to good use. That's the purpose of this book. And the best part is this, anyone can learn these skills.

In the *Water and Fire Survival Handbook*, our goal is to give you the tools, techniques, and "know how" to build shelter, locate and disinfect water for drinking, procure food, and how to build and maintain a fire for boiling, cooking, light, and warmth. Survival has never been about learning unconnected skills; living in isolated little bubbles that will never unite. Survival is based on the use of synergistic skills that work with each other, support each other, and ultimately—buy us one more day of life on Planet Earth.

PART I
WATER

1
The Hazards Involving Water

You may have the wrong idea about finding drinkable water in the wilderness, and I wouldn't be surprised about it at all. For every good example of safe water collection and disinfection, you probably see many more examples of poor, or downright dangerous, water-gathering techniques. Suddenly your mom makes a lot more sense to you. The worst offenders are from movies, television shows, books, and other stories, where adventurous types are often dipping their hands into a creek or river and taking a drink of raw water. Certainly, there are springs and other wild water sources that are still safe to drink without any processing—just as nature intended—and there may have been a time in the distant past when surface water was much cleaner than it is today (or that could be a fantasy, too). But on our dirty planet with an ever-expanding population and increasing pollution, safe surface water is becoming less common every day. In the modern world, even the most remote wilderness areas can have tainted water.

Before we delve into the skills you'll need to locate sources of water and the many different ways you can make it safe for human consumption, it's very important to dispel the myths and clear up the misconceptions surrounding water procurement. It's also helpful to understand the physiological problems that can arise from a lack of water and the harmful organisms and substances that can turn a canteen of water from an asset into a liability. A strong immune system may be able to fight off a few hostile invaders, but why take extra chances especially in an emergency setting? When it comes to the water you drink, like most things, it's better to be safe than sorry.

Dehydration

Before we start worrying about the things in the water that can make us sick, there's an obvious problem that's staring us in the face. It's the problem of running out of water. Every experienced outdoor enthusiast knows they should leave their home with a good amount of drinking water when they set out into nature. But water is heavy (around eight pounds per gallon), and we can hardly carry a week's supply on our backs. Even if we are frugal about our water use, we'll eventually run out of the water we were carrying, and we'll have to decide at some point: Do we try to procure more water or do we go without? Well, here's what happens when you try to survive without enough water: dehydration.

You don't have to be lost in a parched desert to experience dehydration. This deficit of water can happen anywhere, even in a rainforest. In fact, it can happen in any place and in any scenario when your water supply is less that your body's demand. A cold winter outing is an excellent example of these sneaky circumstances. When the weather is freezing and your water bottle is full of ice chunks, you'll be a lot less interested in drinking—even when exerting yourself significantly (like slogging through deep snow). Add in the distraction of a survival situation and dehydration can sneak up on anyone.

Common Symptoms of Dehydration

Dehydration can affect different people in different ways, especially when pre-existing medical conditions and other health problems are a factor. Still, most people suffer from the same symptoms when dehydration creeps over them.

Headache

A lightheaded feeling, some dizziness, and a mild to moderate headache are often the first symptoms you will notice as dehydration starts to set in.

Fatigue

You'll often feel tired and weak as dehydration continues. Your strength and motor skills will drop off, decreasing as your condition worsens and not in conjunction with physical effort. For example, you could feel tired after resting for several hours.

Cottonmouth and Chapped Lips

As thirst builds, you'll experience a dry mouth and your lips may become chapped, especially in cold or dry conditions.

Decreased Urine Output

This is the obvious result of a lack of incoming water. Your body will use and release less water when it's not coming into the body. If you don't need to urinate for hours on end or you only produce a small volume of "darker-than-normal" urine—these are both strong signs that you are getting dehydrated.

Slower Bowels

The symptom of constipation will take a little time to manifest, but it's another sign that your body is shifting into a "water saving" mode. This can range from hard and painful stools that are difficult to evacuate, or more severe constipation.

Difficulty Thinking

Since your brain mainly consists of water, it's easy to become confused due to a lack of water. Dehydration can lead to simple confusion or full delirium, as your mental state deteriorates.

Eyes and Skin

When your skin loses elasticity and your eyes start to look sunken, your skin and eyes are demonstrating a body that is starting to shut down.

Pulse and Blood Pressure

Not only will your blood pressure drop with dehydration, but you may also exhibit a rapid pulse. Together, these conditions put you at risk of shock, and especially endangers people with other health conditions that can be aggravated by this cardiac stress.

Rapid Breathing

Shallow and/or rapid breathing are another symptom of the body trying to compensate for the dangerous condition it is in. Coupled with a high pulse and low blood pressure, it is very likely you will go into shock from dehydration, and immediate medical care is needed.

How to Stop Unnecessary Water Loss

The human body is constantly losing water, even when we are sitting still, sleeping, or otherwise doing nothing—but that doesn't mean you can afford to waste water foolishly. These are some ways to limit your water loss in a survival setting.

Keep Your Mouth Shut

Breathing through your mouth evaporates much more water than breathing through your nostrils. This may not be comfortable for everyone, especially when exerting yourself, but focus on this simple act and you will save water.

Cover Up

Exposed skin loses water much faster than covered skin, so make sure you wear long sleeves, long pants, and even wrap a cloth around your face.

Monitor Your Sweat

Sweating is your body's natural way of cooling you down. It's also your body's way of drying you out. To reduce your need to sweat and save a surprising amount of water, choose cooler times of the day for hard work, and work slower. These will reduce your need to sweat and save a surprising amount of water.

Be Careful with Dry Foods

Certain foods like dried fruit and jerky are great for trail food as they are lightweight and nutritious. But in arid conditions or other situations with limited water, digesting them takes more water from your body than water-rich food, like fresh fruit. As an extra bonus, fresh fruits provide both nutrition and water.

Use Urine Output to Gauge Hydration

Ever wondered if there is an easy guide to determine how much water you should be drinking each day? Well, there is, and you don't even need any special equipment to figure it out. The average person should be drinking at least two quarts a day—more when active or the weather induces sweating. With that much water coming in, you should be urinating nearly that much out except when sweating. You don't have to pee in jugs and measure it, but you should have some sense that you are peeing enough. Urine output can be affected by stress, exertion, health issues, alcohol and caffeine consumption, heat, and many other factors, but in general if you aren't urinating a "normal" volume of light-colored urine every two to three hours, then you need to drink more water. It's just that simple.

Pathogens

The water in that mountain stream was clear and cold. It looked perfectly safe, so you filled your canteen and took a long draught. The water certainly didn't seem dangerous, in fact, it was delicious. There were no traces of the chlorine or other chemicals that you try to ignore in your municipal tap water at home. Hiking farther upstream, you finished the quart and enjoyed the surroundings. Your day in the mountains was going perfectly—until you caught a whiff of decay. Following the stream, you soon came upon a rotting deer carcass lying in the stream bed. The stench was horrible and the maggots wriggled through their feast with enthusiasm. Then you realized the water was actually flowing through the putrid remains—the same water you just drank. And that's how it happens, whether you come across the foul dead animal or not. That cavalier sip of raw water didn't seem like a bad idea at the time, but you soon learned to regret it—the hard way. Plenty of pathogens can taint the water and if your water source carries the wrong organisms into your body, what will happen to you without the assistance of modern medical care? Since safe water can be a life-or-death decision, it's important to understand what you are up against in the wild. Plenty of pathogens can taint the water, and we've organized them into four groups. Here's why we need to disinfect surface water thoroughly and effectively, before we try drinking it.

Viruses

The tiniest of the pathogens, viruses can be present in any surface water source, though they are most common in warmer climates. With more than a hundred known viruses that can infect a human being through drinking water, these organisms can be a real problem. Small enough to slip through many commercially produced water filters, viruses range in size from 0.03 to 0.1 micrometers (a.k.a. microns). That means that these creatures are tiny enough to go inside other tiny pathogenic creatures. Common waterborne viruses include the rotavirus, enterovirus, norovirus, and hepatitis A.

Bacteria

These life forms are microorganisms that vary in size and shape, typically only a few micrometers in length, and appear in spherical, elongated, or spiral shapes. Most are harmless and many are helpful, like the beneficial bacteria in your digestive tract. Some, however, are pathogenic and they can be encountered in waterways—often through feces or dead animals in the water. Waterborne disease-causing bacteria include *Vibrio cholerae*, *Salmonella* spp., *Campylobacter* spp., *Shigella* spp., and *Staphylococcus aureus*.

Protozoa

Protozoa are single-celled animals that are typically microscopic, although a few of the world's species can be large enough to see with the naked eye. Most of these creatures live in water and soil, eating bacteria and other organisms, and causing no harm to humans. A few are even symbiotic, living inside another living thing for mutual advantage. Still others cause a great deal of death and discomfort in the world. Malaria is caused by the *Plasmodium falciparum* species and dysentery can be caused by *Cryptosporidium parvum* and *Giardia lamblia*. Most live in watery conditions when they are not in a host, but they can also form thick-walled cysts that act like shells, allowing them to survive in dry conditions and resist certain disinfectants like chlorine.

Helminths

I don't know why, but I find these simple creatures the creepiest. Helminth is a fancy word for parasitic worms, and you can invite all different sorts of species into your body by drinking contaminated water. The species vary from place to place and their life cycles can play a role in their ability to parasitize a human host. The one consistent thing about these creatures is they can be hard for doctors to diagnose especially once they migrate out of the GI tract and head to greener pastures in your assorted organs. Lungs and livers are the preferred snack for some species, while eyes and brains are the final destination for other revolting worms. To add to the doctors' challenge, some parasites will lie dormant for months or even years before they manifest with strange physical symptoms for the infected person. Some helminths only spend a small part of their life cycle in the water before being released into the fluid in the feces of an infected animal or human. Other helminths stay in water for much of their lives, until the unlucky drinker slurps them up.

Toxins

This issue isn't common in the wilderness but it can occasionally be a problem in the wild and it will definitely be a problem in the wake of a disaster. There are more dangers than just living organisms in the surface water of the world, and these are some of the common threats you'll face in an emergency which requires you to find your own water.

Toxic Elements

Old mining areas and industrial areas are likely places for toxic elements in the ground water. In my home area, gold miners once used mercury to clump gold dust together, and as a result, these mining areas have high mercury levels to this day. Some of the most common pollutants are arsenic, cadmium, chromium, copper, nickel, lead, and mercury. They may naturally release into the water from raw ore in the ground, but are more frequently introduced into waterways as a pollutant when dispersed from industry in the form of smokestacks releasing it into the air, and cooling or wash water being released into waterways around a factory. It's best to know the history of an area, if possible, before relying on a water source on a regular basis. Occasional trace amounts of these elements won't be likely to cause any health concerns, but steady consumption over a long period can bring on all sorts of health risks.

Pesticides

In a 1999 study in California, over a dozen pesticides were found in California's drinking water sources. While the volume of pest control chemicals in two quarts of water was many times less than the volume of chemicals on the average daily consumption of fruits and vegetables, it's still unnerving to know that both the food and water are contaminated in one of the strictest states in America. This would make ponds and lakes that are downhill of conventional agricultural areas less ideal as water sources.

Other Chemicals

In the wake of a hurricane or some other natural disaster, more than just pesticides end up in the flood waters. Industry and infrastructures, like chemical storage facilities, sewage plants, garbage dumps, and storm water systems, can be destroyed, sending unimaginable filth into the local waterways. Not only are the waters tainted with fecal matter containing viruses, bacteria, protozoa, parasites, household chemical waste, and excreted drug products, we also face the toxic chemicals that are released when industrial buildings and storage facilities are overwhelmed by flooding. This witch's brew of flood water will not be a viable water source and it will contaminate the area for a long time to come. Worse still, some entities dump chemicals and waste into waterways intentionally and not as a result of a disaster. To avoid the poisons released accidentally and on purpose, it's best to find emergency water sources "upstream" and away from factories and industrial areas.

The Most Dangerous Water in the Desert

When you come upon a water source that's surrounded by dead animals and their bones, your survival instincts should be raising all the "red flags" in your brain. However, it's not always the case that a dangerous water source will present such an obvious warning sign. One common toxin in desert regions is arsenic. Over thousands of years, native populations have developed metabolic processes to tolerate dangerous levels of arsenic. Unfortunately, this isn't a trait we can develop overnight. The indigenous people of Chile's Atacama Desert are able to break down arsenic into two relatively harmless compounds, which is a vital attribute in the world's driest non-polar desert. The levels of arsenic in the water of this region can exceed 1 milligram per quart, over a hundred times the World Health Organization's safe limits. Even low levels of arsenic increase cancer risks, contribute to cardiovascular disease, and affect the skin. You won't be able to see, taste, or smell small amounts of this toxic element, but very high levels may create a "garlic" scent or flavor in the water.

Saltwater and Related Fluids

The average patch of ocean water contains about 3.5 percent salt, consisting mainly of sodium chloride, which affects the density of seawater and its freezing point. It also affects us humans when we try to drink seawater. While our cells require sodium as a necessary nutrient for chemical balances and reactions, drinking this overly salty liquid, instead of fresh water, floods our bodies and cells with too much salt. With saltwater as our only beverage, our bodies struggle to find an equilibrium. Our kidneys are only able to make urine that is less salty than saltwater. Over time, this means that we end up urinating more fluid than we consumed in an effort to rid ourselves of excess salt. Over days or weeks, this leads to dehydration and eventually death (if you last that long). Other health issues can also be exacerbated by too much salt. Finally, the severe electrolyte imbalance in your brain can cause an otherwise healthy person to make deadly errors in judgment. For example, people have been documented jumping out of perfectly good life rafts into shark-filled waters, after only drinking seawater for a few days. Similarly, drinking urine or blood—both full of assorted salts—will also cause you to urinate more liquid than you should, over-salt your cells, and can even be a source of pathogens, which are all the more dangerous to you in your weakened state. To sum it up simply, if it's salty—don't drink it.

Water-Gathering Myths

Sometimes, and I'm always surprised when it happens, pop culture resources get a survival skill right. But most of the time, they don't. Here are some common water-related myths and real-world solutions.

The animals are drinking it raw, so I can too.

Nope, humans have a very unique and very long gastrointestinal tract with plenty of twists and turns for parasites and pathogens to snuggle in and build a new home. Even though other mammals are drinking directly from a water source, it doesn't mean that you can get away with it. Instead, you could follow animals to the water they drink, then collect it and process it to make it safe.

Chop open a cactus, they're full of water.

Sure, that works in cartoons, but have you tried it in real life? Most cacti species are full of bitter gelatinous pulp or dry mealy pith. They are not barrels of water sitting in the desert and waiting for you to chop off the top. Don't get the wrong idea. Many cacti are useful in a survival situation. Some produce edible fruits, while others give us stout needles to use for tools or traps. You can even add the cactus pulp to a solar still or some other piece of improvised distillation equipment to extract some of the water they contain. In Chapter Two, we'll take a look at some of the plants that actually do offer drinkable liquid water. Just make sure you use a local plant ID guide to make certain you have the right species and nothing toxic.

Don't drink your water, you should ration it.

There are situations where rationing water makes a lot of sense, yet people have also died from holding out too long. Yes, you don't want to overhydrate in any survival situation so that you are peeing too often and too clear. But you also don't want to ration your water so far that you end up dehydrated. A better gambit might be to "ration your sweat" instead of your water. What we mean by that is to limit your water loss. As mentioned in Chapter One, this can be done by limiting your physical exertion during the hottest part of the day, trying to breathe just through your nose, and wearing thin, light-colored clothing in hot sunny environments. Don't wait until dehydration has a hold on you before you implement these water saving moves.

People only die of dehydration in the desert.

The deserts of the world certainly exemplify the conditions in which a person could die of thirst, but any place on earth can be the backdrop to this hazard. Forests and grasslands of every kind and even snowy wastes and swamps can lead people to a similar fate. People don't like to drink muddy water or water with chunks of ice in it, and they ignore their body's urgent need for liquid. People who are severely injured or ill may also lose the fight against dehydration, through vomiting, diarrhea, and fever. Wherever you are, the best way to keep track of your hydration and prevent dehydration is to monitor your water intake and urine output. Do this, don't be too picky about your water sources, and disinfect the water properly—and you'll likely survive to tell the tale.

2
Locating Water

Now that you know the dangers of dehydration and you've learned some of the hazardous things that may be present in raw surface water, it's time to look at the multitude of places where water can be located and collected. Some of the most obvious and frequently used resources, like waterways and rainfall, can be found right in front of your nose. But these aren't the only providers of drinking water. Even the driest terrains, like arid deserts and isolated mountaintops can harbor their own surprising water resources. Yes, even the Sahara Desert has water sources, though finding an oasis may be trickier than you'd ever imagine. To take full advantage of all practical water sources, you'll have to learn the particulars of each landscape, and asking questions before your adventure will help. How do seasonal weather patterns affect surface water availability? How do the land features influence the water table and surface water? Should you go uphill or downhill for water in a desert environment? I hope you don't have to learn the answers to these questions the hard way. It's impossible to know how many people have died through the ages while wandering in clueless circles, hoping to find water in the wrong place. But in those same conditions, the people who knew how to read nature's clues were often the ones who could find the surface water and live to tell the tale. Modern people are very spoiled. We have access to fresh clean drinking water in developed countries at the turn of a faucet. Water is a precious commodity, and it's one that we never fully appreciate until we must find it for ourselves.

Finding Water on the Landscape

With abundant rainfall spread over a water-rich landscape, finding something to drink isn't too hard. Conversely, after a period of little rain and in drier climates, locating water in the wilderness can be a life-or-death struggle. Those are the times when you'll need every trick in the book to find water in the wild.

Go with the Flow

Since the rain and natural drainages are always going to follow a predictable path downhill, in most areas it's a good strategy to walk to a lower elevation to find water. As you go, look for landscape features that direct water. Springs in the ground and rainfall aren't ever going to run uphill. They will be funneled downhill, pulled by gravity and directed by landforms. So, walk downhill, looking for natural drainages like gullies, draws, and valleys—and you will often be able to follow these features to a creek or some other water source at a lower elevation. Of course, the water table and weather play a major role in water availability, but going downhill is the most practical plan. The alternative, often reserved for dry climates, is to head uphill. Natural water springs are the source of most creeks and rivers, and these emerge from the ground in places where the water table is high. By checking the bottom of large rock outcroppings, the bases of cliffs, or higher areas in ravines, you can sometimes find a spring bubbling to the surface. And after you've made your way uphill or downhill to find a spring, stream, river, or lake, remember that all surface water should be considered contaminated and disinfected before drinking. The one possible exception is spring water. If you have no way to disinfect your water, springs are usually the safest surface water source to drink raw. Catch the water as it flows out of its source, not farther down.

Dig for Water

In the event that you followed the terrain down but only found a dry creek bed instead of flowing water on the surface, you can try digging for water. Look for the lowest spot in the bed, checking for the dampest soil or sand. With your available tools, or even a stick, begin digging a hole. When the color changes and the soil is obviously moister, keep digging. If the hole stays dry, try another spot. With luck, dirty water will begin to seep into the hole. This is called a seep well and all you have to do now is wait for the water to collect. This muddy water can be boiled for safety and drunk as soon as it cools, though a nicer approach is to wait for the water to collect and the mud to settle. Seep wells are especially useful and important in dry coastal areas, like sand dunes. Without a fresh water source at the beach or island, and since you can't drink salt water, you can dig a series of seep wells beyond the beach dunes. Look for the lowest place behind the first or second dune. Dig a hole and wait for the water. You may find a layer of fresh water if you don't dig too deep. This is rainfall that has been collected by the landforms and protected from evaporation by the sand. Be careful not to dig too deep before allowing water to seep in, as you may dig right down to the salty ground water. This trick doesn't always work and tidal water movement can have a major impact on the presence of fresh water. Try it anyway. It's the only way to find out for sure. Experiment with the depth of the holes, their location, and timing of the digging as the tide can play a role. If it's salty, try again—if it's not salty, you did it!

Use Precipitation as a Water Source

In all its different forms, precipitation can bring us water. This can be obvious and easy, like leaving a container out in the rain; or it can be more work, like collecting and melting snow. Familiar precipitation forms like rain, snow, sleet, ice, and hail can all be collected as water sources, rain being the easiest of the bunch. Frozen forms of precipitation present us with additional challenges. When the weather is cold enough for snow, ice, or sleet, it is also cold enough to give a person hypothermia. And even though we may observe wildlife eating snow for hydration, it's not a safe practice for humans. Because it's so fluffy, you'd have to eat ten quarts of snow to have one quart of melted water in your stomach. Chilling your mouth, throat, stomach, and body core with ten quarts of snow is a sure way to become hypothermic. The right approach in freezing or very cold temperatures is to melt your frozen precipitation and ideally warm it up before drinking any of it. And in the case of old snow that has been lying around for days, weeks, or months, it's smart to boil the water or use some other means of disinfection, as it may have been contaminated by animals while it was on the ground. Dew and frost are also forms of precipitation that can be gathered. Use a piece of cloth—the more absorbent, the better—to swab up these water sources from the landscape. The cloth can be dry for dew, as the dew will wet it. You'll have the best luck sopping up dew in low-lying areas late in the night or very early in the morning. Wipe it up from grass, rocks, or any other surface where it collects. It will be swimming with dirt, dust, insect droppings, and many other filthy things, so make sure you disinfect dew and frost before drinking it. Use a wet cloth for frost, as the wet cloth will melt the frost. This will be too dirty to drink directly but it can be wrung out into a container and disinfected.

Collect Drinking Water from Vegetation

Many different plants found around the world, such as banana trees and certain types of bamboo, can provide water for much of the year. In North America, however, plant sources of water tend to only be available for the first six months of each year.

Try a Drink of Tree Sap

Certain deciduous tree saps provide one of the most predictable and high-volume sources of water from the plant kingdom. The dates of the "sap runs" will vary with the temperatures of the season, elevation, and latitude. In my home area of the mid-Atlantic, the sap starts running in mid-winter (typically late January or early February). Farther north, it won't start until a month later. The temperature is the main factor in this variability. The sap will flow when the nights are below freezing and the days are above freezing, and the peak of the sap run will last for several days or a week. During this brief window, it's possible to get up to a gallon per day from just one tap. Most trees do not produce drinkable sap, but the most useful species include the maples (the genus *Acer*), sycamore trees (*Platanus occidentalis*), birches (the genus *Betula*), walnuts (the genus *Juglans*) and hickories (the genus *Carya*). The water is cold, clear, full of minerals, and slightly sweet thanks to the sugar content. You don't have to worry about boiling or treating the water, either. Wood is a natural water filter, removing bacteria and pathogens as the sap flows through it. It only takes one cubic centimeter of woody tissue to filter out bacteria like E. coli, and the sap will pass through many feet of wood as it makes its way from the tips of the roots and up the trunk of the tree. Each of the species mentioned above provides sugar, between 2 and 5 percent by volume, acting as a pre-sweetened beverage and being suitable to boil down for delicious syrup. This is where real maple syrup comes from. Harvest your own sap in the right season and ideally on trees over a foot in diameter, by drilling a hole through the bark and into the trunk wood a few inches. Insert a tube to direct the fluid into some kind of container. Optimal results occur when you tap a healthy tree on the sunny side of the trunk, above a large root or below a large branch. Keep the sap cold and drink it or boil it down within a week. It will sour if kept in a warm location or kept too long.

Maple and other trees can produce large volumes of watery sap but only during a short window of time in late winter.

Collect Grape Vine Water

In the springtime, the sap starts flowing in North American grape vines (the genus *Vitis*), which produce water when cut. Any size of vine may be used but larger ones will produce better than small vines. For smaller specimens, use a sharp knife or similar tool to chop off the vine at an angle a few feet away from the ground. For arm thick vines, chop a notch into them. From small vines you'll get dripping water, which could provide many ounces of water over a period of hours (before the wound "clots"). From large vines, water can gush out as if a faucet was opened. Use an identification guide to make a 100 percent positive identification that the vine is a grape vine. North American species aren't the only ones with water. Certain tropical grape species (also called "water vines") provide water throughout Central America and the Caribbean. The best species is the Caribbean grape (*Vitis tiliifolia*). This species offers sap for a longer season than North American grapes, allowing you to cut the vine and drink the water over a span of months.

Squeeze Some Berries

During the summer months, juice can be pressed from edible berries and used as a drink. Raspberries, blueberries, mulberries, blackberries, and similar edible berries and fruits can be crushed and placed in the center of a clean cloth. By gathering up the cloth and twisting, you can wring out the juice for healthy hydration as well as vitamins, minerals and calories. It's like an all-natural sports drink! When both food and water are lacking, drinking only the juice prevents us from having to pass seeds and other indigestible materials through our digestive tract thus saving a little more water.

Drink Coconut Water

In tropical and sub-tropical environments, water can be collected from green coconuts. Each of these will provide roughly twelve ounces of safe, clean water. Sealed inside the shells, this water will stay drinkable for weeks. In addition to hydration, coconut water also provides some caloric value (mainly sugar) and a good dose of potassium. The only drawback is that you need to limit your consumption. Drinking much more than two green coconuts per day might result in diarrhea, and you may actually lose water.

Create Your Own Distillation Equipment

While it's rarely quick to set up, you can fashion your own improvised distillation equipment from commonly available supplies. The most basic way to set up a survival distillation method is the "solar still," which collects water from the soil, desalinates salt water, and to some extent disinfects the water. It's not usually going to produce gallons of cold water, but it will produce ounces of hot dirt-flavored water that is generally safe to drink without further processing. Manage your expectations accordingly—some water is much better than none. To make one, you'll need a piece of clear or milky plastic sheeting at least a few feet wide. Black trash bags and other light blocking plastic won't work. You'll also need a tool to dig a large hole in the ground and a clean container to place in the hole as a water catch. Dig the hole as large as your plastic sheeting allows, several feet wide and deep would be ideal. The shape of the pit can vary but it should match the size and shape of the plastic that will be covering it. The pit should also be in a damp area and it must be in full sunlight. Place some of the excess dirt in piles near the pit but not right at the edges. Set your container in the center of the bottom of the pit and cover the pit with the plastic sheeting. Use loose dirt to "seal" the plastic down around the perimeter of the pit to make an airtight seal, allowing the plastic to sag a little as you work. The plastic should not be tight across the pit like the head of a drum since you'll be making a cone shape from it next. Use a small smooth stone or a little dirt to weigh down the middle of the loose plastic sheeting, pulling it tight and making a cone shape. Align the weight on the plastic so that it is right over the container. Now you wait. The sun shining through the clear or milky plastic will cause the evaporation of moisture from the soil and any water that seeped or you poured into the pit. As this steam collects on the cooler plastic, it condenses and trickles down into your container. In a few hours, you'll have a few ounces of water. Pouring salty or brackish water into the pit will increase the yield and will naturally desalinate the water since salt can't rise up in the steam.

Make a Transpiration Bag

Don't have a big piece of clear plastic to make a solar still? You can make a scaled-down version of this steam-condensing invention if you have a large clear plastic bag. Identify some non-toxic shrubs or trees in the area and pick out a particularly leafy branch in the sunlight. Place the bag over the branch and use string or tape to bind the mouth of the bag tightly against the twig. If the branch droops downward, nothing extra must be done. If the branch sticks outward or upward, place a small clean stone in the bag to create a "pocket" where water can collect. Plants naturally expel water vapor, which collects in the bag. In several hours, the vapor will collect and condense into liquid water. You won't get much and it will likely taste bitter from the natural tannins that come out of the leaves touching the bag, but the technique does yield water.

Prepare Your Watercraft

The paradox is almost painful. You're surrounded by water yet dying of thirst. For those who may find themselves adrift in a salty body of water, it's very important to prepare your emergency supplies with water collection in mind. Since salt water isn't safe for human consumption, you should pack a supply of drinking water, and you'll also need some type of equipment to separate the salt from fresh water when your packaged water runs out. The three main products in the marine marketplace today are inflatable solar stills, reverse osmosis pumps, and forward osmosis bags. The solar stills blow up like a little raft and have a conical clear plastic top. They can be tied off to your life raft or used on the deck of boats. After filling the reservoir with sea water, the sun will turn it into steam, and it will condense inside the unit. The second option is a reverse osmosis hand pump. These are similar to hand pump water filters and they remove both pathogens and salt. The third option is the forward osmosis bag. These draw a small amount of water through a membrane. They are inexpensive but they only process a small amount of water and can only be used once or a limited number of times at a push.

Using Unorthodox Water Sources

The reason we are out of water may not always be that we are stuck in a wilderness survival situation. In fact, you're far more likely to face a water shortage in the wake of a serious storm or natural disaster than you are to run out of water while you are lost in the wild. The solution may be as simple as hopping in the car and heading to a store to buy drinks outside the affected area. But in certain cases, that won't be an option. Flooding is one of the strangest and ironic disasters. In a flood you are surrounded by water that isn't safe to drink unless it can be distilled. Flood waters often contain every form of biological and chemical contamination that your area can dish out. Just think of all the sewage plants, animal farms, industrial areas, and garbage dumps that are covered by a flood—adding their filth to the witch's brew of muddy water around you. Here is what you can do in this situation and other scenarios in which your normal water supply is cut off:

Finding Water in Homes and Businesses

Even when the power is out and the municipal water supply has stopped flowing, there's water hidden in the average home and business.

The Water Heater

This large tank of water is a common fixture in most homes and businesses. Whether they are heated with electricity or gas, they contain many gallons of the same water you were drinking before the disaster. Since the incoming and outgoing pipes are on the top of the tank, there will be water held inside even when the pipes run dry. This water can be accessed by the valve on the side of the tank, near the bottom. The first water that comes out will likely be dirty looking, filled with rust and sediment, but the water should run clear after that. If the water outage is recent, you can use the water as is. Use a disinfecting process if the water has been sitting for a few days or longer, as the warm water may grow bacteria.

The Toilet Tank

While it's hardly appetizing, the water tank on the back of every toilet also contains water from the same supply you were drinking before. If there are no chemicals like disinfecting tablets, bowl cleaners, or scents added to the water in the tank, it is safe to drink.

Exterior Faucets

In urban areas, many businesses have an outdoor water spigot. By design, these do not have a typical handle in order to prevent unauthorized use. Yet most home improvement stores sell "four-way" water keys, which can act as a handle for the most used water faucet valves. Add this small tool to your urban survival kit or vehicle emergency kit and you may be able to get water during a disaster.

3
Water Disinfection Methods

You've located a water source but your fight against dehydration isn't over. There's one more battle to win. You'll have to disinfect the water before it is safe to drink. Even though the environment may provide many sources of water that are clean enough to drink without disinfection, you should still assume that every water source is teeming with microscopic life (because it probably is). Many of these organisms are harmless and some are even beneficial in your gastrointestinal tract, but unless you have a microscope and the time to check every single drop before consumption (unlikely), you won't really know what you are imbibing. By consuming just a few of the "wrong" organisms, you'll have a breeding population that will try to take over your guts and create a new civilization inside your body. When your sickened body can't hold them back anymore, they will burst forth and seek out new hosts to "colonize" and the cycle continues. Due to the filthy conditions that constantly inoculated our ancestors, they could probably tolerate plenty of harmful organisms in their bodies or they died early. Modern people, however, are spoiled by the abundance of clean water, disinfected food, and sanitized surfaces. This has rendered us more vulnerable to many of our old water-borne foes, so all due caution should be taken. As you'll see in this chapter, there are many ways to kill the creatures that are swimming through raw water sources and you'll want to use the right one for the job. Some methods will work on water in any condition, while other methods require the water to be within certain parameters. For example, the water must be clear for UV disinfection.

Learn About Your Options

Even on a day-to-day basis, we can't afford to make mistakes with the safety of our drinking water. This care and caution will be even more important when we are forced to disinfect our own drinking water in an emergency. One simple mistake could leave us very ill, so we must get everything right. Fortunately, we have many options when it comes to killing or removing the dangerous organisms that drift through our local waterways and float in our collected water. These are some of the primary methods for water disinfection in a survival setting.

Boiling

The most basic (and ancient) form of disinfection is boiling the water in a fireproof container. This can be done over the fire or beside the fire.

Chemical Disinfection

Numerous chemicals can be added to raw water in an effort to kill pathogenic organisms. Common products like iodine tablets and chlorine tablets are easy to use and carry. Certain household and first aid products can also provide us with safe drinking water.

Water Filtration

Factory made water filters come in all shapes and styles, and even the cheapest one on the market will screen out many of the pathogens in a raw water source. DIY filters can also be used to clarify raw water before passing it through a commercial filter or using some other disinfection method.

Solar Disinfection

The sun's harmful rays can do more than just burn your skin. Ultraviolet light can also kill or disable pathogens when they are exposed to a strong and lengthy dose.

Commercial UV Disinfection

Producing a strong blast of ultraviolet light, UV disinfection "pens" and similar devices can be used to disinfect small batches of clear water. This technology can provide us with a backup to other water treatment plans, and the smaller versions are handy for travelers since the devices are small and fast acting.

Boiling Water for Disinfection

When it comes to simplicity and effectiveness, it's hard to beat the ancient disinfection technique of boiling water. By placing your raw water in a fireproof container and bringing the water to a rolling boil for at least five minutes, the heat will kill the four major groups of harmful waterborne organisms. The boiling method isn't perfect, as this method doesn't remove salt, radiation, certain types of pollution, or mud, but you can say goodbye to the bacteria, viruses, parasites, and protozoa that would try to set up camp in your intestines. Boiling works on both clear and muddy water and it can be accomplished by using a metal pot, pan, or bowl placed right beside the bed of coals in a fire, or suspended over a fire, which will boil the water more quickly.

Boil Water with Hot Rocks

When you have a metal pot, a water source, and the ability to make a fire, boiling your drinking water for safety is simple. But what happens when you don't have a metal pot for boiling? Our ancestors figured this out before the metal pot was even invented. The use of hot stones for boiling, cooking, and keeping warm dates back millennia and this ancient technique can still serve us today. If our only containers are a wooden bowl or depressions in large rocks, we can't use these over a fire for boiling. The wooden vessel would catch fire and crack, spilling our precious water onto the fire and costing us everything. The water would be gone, the wooden bowl would be ruined, and the fire would probably be extinguished. Things aren't easier when holding water in a stone cavity. A depression in a boulder can't exactly be moved, and if the rock is small enough to be mobile, the depression probably won't hold much water. Even if you could mount the cavity-bearing rock over your fire, the small amount of water would likely evaporate away before it was hot enough to boil. So, here's the alternative: By heating up stones to a "red hot" temperature, you can drop them into vessels of water that can't be used over the fire. These containers can vary a great deal. Dry hollow gourds and large wooden bowls are traditional rock-boiling containers. Carefully folded tree bark containers are another option. You could even carve out the side of a log to make a larger basin or use an immobile cavity like a depression in a boulder or even a hole in clay-rich ground. Try it yourself by collecting about two dozen small stones from a dry location. These should be about the size of golf balls and only collected from dry sites. Place these stones in the heart of a normal-sized campfire and heat them for 30 to 45 minutes. While they heat up, you can collect your water and bring it near the fire, and you can create a pair of tongs to grab the hot rocks, which will be over 1000° Fahrenheit after being heated for the allotted time. The easiest way to make tongs is to tie two flexible sticks together. This apparatus allows you to pick out hot rocks from the fire as if you were using a huge set of tweezers. Keep in mind that picking up hot rocks with any tool (especially an improvised tool) can be quite dangerous. Practice gripping and moving unheated stones before you try red-hot rocks for the first time. When ready, pick out one rock and carefully blow off any excess ashes. Drop the rock into your water vessel and watch it bubble and steam. Remove the rock when it stops hissing and add a new hot rock. Continue to cycle fresh rocks into the water vessel and the water will soon boil. After boiling for five minutes, the water will be as safe as it can be. It's still possible to get live organisms in the water as the rocks only boil the body of water and don't bring the edges of the vessel to a high heat, which can cross-contaminate your boiled water. Still, this is your best shot at clean water when you have no metal, glass, clay, or stone containers that can be used over the fire. There's also another use for rock boiling. You can use the technique to brew some tea or make soup. This is as much a primitive cooking technique as it is a water disinfection method.

WARNING!

You should only collect rocks from a dry location if you'll be placing them into a fire. Rocks collected in and around the water may be filled with water. For example, the waterlogged rocks you'd collect at a beach, along a river, or in any other wet area may have water trapped deep inside the stone. As the heat of the fire conducts into the rock, the water inside the rock will transform into steam. The result can be a powerful explosion that sends sharp rock fragments flying in every direction at a dangerous velocity. If you want to test unknown types of stone, toss some samples into a large fire and then retreat at least fifty feet away. Watch the fire to see if anything explodes within it and listen for loud pops. Allow the fire to die down naturally and inspect the rocks lying in the ashes. If nothing blew up and the rocks didn't crumble into sand, then you've selected a good type of stone for rock boiling.

Use a "Found" Container

You may be caught without a pot to boil the water but you'll usually find trash in even the most pristine wilderness areas on Earth. Discarded glass bottles, aluminum beverage cans, and steel food cans will provide alternative boiling vessels for water disinfection. These should be cleaned as best as possible. An easy way to do this is to pour a little water, some sand, and some tiny stones inside the container. Cover the opening and shake the container to scour the insides. Rinse the vessel clean and fill it with raw water. Set the vessel at the edge of the ashes close beside the fire and it will begin to heat up. Depending on the size of your fire, the water may start to boil in about ten minutes. Allow it to boil for a minimum of five minutes (after the boil begins), then cool it before drinking.

Using Chemicals to Make Your Drinking Water Safe

When you drink water from a municipal water supply, your safety is assured thanks to chemical water disinfection among other practices. This is also what's happening when you add disinfecting chemicals to the raw water you collect from the environment. Here's how to perform your own small-scale water disinfection with commonly available chemicals and products:

Buy Disinfection Tablets

One of the most dependable and easiest methods of chemical disinfection is to use commercially available water disinfection tablets. These are a great option for travelers, hikers, and backpackers. These products are also a great fit for vehicle emergency kits, survival kits, and bug out bags. The two main options for chemical disinfection tablets are iodine tablets

Iodine tablets offer fast and dependable water disinfection.

and chlorine-based tablets. The iodine tablets generally have a one-year shelf life, a more metallic taste, and are not recommended for anyone with a shellfish allergy, nursing moms, or those who are pregnant. The other option for tablet disinfection on a small scale is the chlorine-based tablet. These generally have a longer shelf life and are more widely tolerated, though they take several hours to achieve maximum effectiveness while iodine tablets make the water safe to drink in less than 45 minutes.

Try Ordinary Bleach

This is often a surprise for most people, but ordinary household bleach can be safely used to disinfect raw water. This should be plain bleach, the same product you'd use on white laundry. It should not have added scents or strange features like the thick viscosity of "splash-less" bleach. Ordinary bleach is the product you want, and it should be less than six months old as older bleach has lost chlorine due to evaporation. You'll also want to make sure you read the label and look at the active ingredient before you add this product to your drinking water for an "off label" use. Many companies produce laundry bleach that is 5.25 or 6 percent sodium hypochlorite although a few have gone to a higher percentage. When using bleach in the 5.25 to 6 percent range, you'll add two to four drops of this chlorine bleach to each quart of water. If, however, your product is a more "concentrated" bleach solution—somewhere around 8 percent sodium hypochlorite—keep the minimum safe dose at two drops of bleach per quart of water and lower your maximum dose to three drops of bleach per quart of water. Whatever the bleach concentration, colder water and sediment-laden water require more bleach than warm water or clear water. Once you've determined how much bleach to use and double checked your numbers, add the drops of bleach to your raw water and shake it until well mixed. Place the bottle in a dark location or at least out of direct sunlight for one hour.

After the time has passed, open the water bottle and check the scent. You should be able to smell the bleach somewhat. If you were uncertain about the dose of bleach, for example, the water was very cold but you only added 3 drops of 5.25 percent bleach, add another drop of bleach—being careful not to exceed the maximum dose—shake it up, and allow the water to sit for another hour.

Disinfect with Iodine

The iodine solution in your first aid kit can protect your wounds from infection. The same solution can also protect you from waterborne pathogens. The two most common forms of iodine are tincture of iodine 2 percent and povidone iodine 10 percent (often sold under the brand name Betadine). Don't be confused by the percentages. That bottle of tincture of iodine 2 percent is a different formula from povidone iodine 10 percent solution and the tincture is stronger. You will only need to drip five to ten drops of tincture of iodine 2 percent into one quart of water. Why the range of variance? Ideal water that is clear and not too cold will not need as much iodine, so only five drops are necessary for clear warm water. When the water is cloudy with sediment or very cold, the iodine can be absorbed by the sediment particles and slowed down by the frigid temperatures. You'll need to drop ten drops of tincture of iodine 2 percent into ice cold or cloudy water. If the water is somewhere between these extremes, you'll have to make a judgment call and split the difference. Seven or eight drops may be the right amount for water that is in between. Similarly, 10 percent povidone iodine solution has a range based on water clarity and temperature. Use eight drops per quart of warm and clear water. Add sixteen drops per quart of water that is very cold or cloudy. These drops can be added with an eye dropper or carefully dripped off the edge of a spoon or the bottle cap. Allow the water bottle to sit in the shade for one hour and then drink.

Don't Get Tricked by Cross-Contamination

Once you've added your chosen chemicals to the water, you'll want to replace the bottle lid and shake the bottle to dissolve tablets and mix liquids. The next thing you'll want to do is flush the cap and wipe down the bottle, to avoid cross-contamination from a dirty cap, bottle threads, or the bottle exterior. This can be done by turning the bottle upside down and unscrewing the cap just enough for a little water to flow out (don't spill too much water). Use this chemical-laden water to wipe down the bottle exterior and you'll be as safe as you can get.

Buy a Filter

There are many commercially available water filters on the market today. Manufacturers are providing us with some great options and technology including ceramic filter elements, carbon filters, hollow fiber filters, and many others. These products provide disinfection by filtration, and some provide extra disinfection through some kind of pathogen killing aspect like silver or iodine. Handheld pumps, gravity-fed "bag filters," and suck-through "survival straws" are just a few of your choices in the marketplace. Most of these are small and portable, though a few are larger and designed for a base camp or homestead setting. For example, a company called Berkey makes several versions of gravity-fed tabletop units that are so easy to use, a child could operate them. These tabletop filters work by pouring raw water in a reservoir on top of the unit, and the water seeps through the filter cartridge(s) into a holding tank below. Better for the trail, hand pump filters are made by many different manufacturers, ranging in size from personal use to group applications. Some units are more affordable, some are more expensive, but the main difference between water filters is their filtration cartridge. This is the heart of the unit, and they are made from different materials and combinations of materials. A straight carbon filter, for example, will screen out most pathogens (especially the larger ones) and it can absorb numerous pollutants from chlorine and lead to iron and PCBs. The downside of carbon is that it can be easily clogged when filtering muddy water. By contrast, synthetic fiber filters are made from hollow plastic tubes packed into a tight formation. These filters can easily screen out larger pathogens, but not chemical pollution. If a fiber filter becomes clogged with mud or silt, it can typically be flushed backwards to clear it. My personal favorite of all is the ceramic filter. These don't remove as much pollution as a carbon filter, but they typically remove pathogens more effectively. Ceramic filters can usually be maintained in the field and provide a very long lifespan. The best ceramic filters have silver particles or other antimicrobial

Commercially available water filters provide the fastest method of water disinfection.

elements integrated into the ceramic. This can kill the tiniest pathogens (like viruses), while most other filters cannot remove or kill them.

Make a Cloth Pre-Filter

The clothes on your back can do more than shield you from sun and shame. Many kinds of fabric are used around the world to filter water, and science is just now starting to pay attention. The ancient tradition of cloth water filters may date back to the earliest use of cloth (at least 8000 years old). A recent NIH study performed in Bangladesh showed that the use of cloth water filters reduced the cases of cholera by nearly half when raw river water was filtered in four layers of cloth. Additional testing showed that old cloth was the key. As the fabric was used, the strands in the weave became fuzzier, making them a more effective filter element. In the best results, four layers of worn cotton fabric filtered out as much as 99 percent of all cholera bacteria. Even though this isn't a perfect system, by pouring raw water through stacked layers of cloth, we can reduce the number of pathogens that our immune system would have to fight off. It's important to emphasize that you shouldn't trust your safety to cloth filtration alone, but when you are unable to boil water, use chemicals, or perform other disinfection methods, the use of cloth filters is better than nothing.

Create Your Own Tripod Filter

If you have a little spare cloth that you can cut up, plus a few sticks, string, and some natural filter elements, you can make your own water filter to improve the clarity and taste of muddy, silty, swampy, or otherwise vile water sources. The tripod filter is usually created using a tripod of sticks as a frame, with layers of grass, charcoal, and sand as filtration elements. This device can be set up in a camp or moved from site to site as needed, and while it won't filter out all the pathogens from raw water sources, it does improve water quality by removing mud and debris. Begin building your tripod filter by lashing together three sticks, each one about four and a half feet (1.5 m) long. Stand the tripod up and open the legs equally for strength and stability. The next step is to tie in three pieces of triangular cloth. These should match the dimensions of the tripod, stacked one above the other. You'll need a small one for the top, a medium one in the middle and a large one at the bottom. In the top piece of cloth (the smallest one), make a tight nest of fresh green grass. The leaves of fresh grass are covered in tiny barbs, which can catch dirt and debris in the water. To the second layer of the filter, add crushed black charcoal from a fire. Avoid using dusty charcoal powder as it will clog the filter, or large charcoal chunks, as they don't have enough surface area. Only use tiny chunks of crushed charcoal. Last but not least, fill the bottom layer of the filter with clean sand. This will grab even more particles and provide the bulk of the unit's filtration. Take a test run by pouring raw water onto the top layer of the filter and allow the water to slowly run through the filter unit. Initially, you'll see a lot of charcoal dust coming out in the water along with dirt from the sandy filter layer. Once this is flushed out, however, the water will begin to run more clearly. Slowly pour the raw water into the top layer and allow the water to flow through the three layers at a consistent speed. Collect the water in a vessel underneath the filter and perform some additional method of disinfection (like boiling the water) to ensure that it's safe to drink. Make sure this device fits your needs by considering these benefits and problems before you build a tripod filter.

Benefits

- Even a filter this rough can clear the water and improve it.
- You can build it from a wide variety of common materials.

- By removing the filter elements, the filter becomes reuseable.
- By taking out heavy materials, the filter becomes portable.

Problems

- Without cloth or some similar porous material, it's hard to build.
- If you can't make fire you won't have easy access to charcoal.
- Fresh green grass is a seasonal material and not always available.
- Tripod filters don't remove enough pathogens to make the water safe to drink without additional processes.

Disinfecting with Sunlight

The harmful UV rays in sunlight aren't just damaging to our skin and eyes, they are capable of damaging waterborne pathogens too. If enough organisms are killed or disabled in a raw water source, the water is essentially disinfected and much safer to drink than before. The technique has been called SODIS and SOLDIS (which are both short for "solar disinfection") and it's being used as a water disinfection method in struggling parts of the world and in survival situations. The best part of the method is that you don't need specialized equipment or chemicals to do it. You don't even need fuel to burn, as you would with boiling. You just need to find some clear water as the technique isn't reliable with muddy or cloudy water. You'll also need to focus on clarity. For best results, you will need to find a clear plastic bag or clear plastic bottle, up to two liters in size. The bottle cannot be scratched up or dirty and it cannot be glass or made from milky plastic as these all block UV rays. The last part of the recipe is the sun. Eight full hours of direct sunlight or two full days of cloudy but not rainy weather will expose the water to enough UV light that most (or possibly all) of the waterborne pathogens will be dead or disabled. It's important to note that SOLDIS works better in equatorial areas and becomes less effective as you travel away from the equator.

Use a UV Device

Now that you know what UV light can do to the pathogens swimming in your prospective water, you can have a greater appreciation for a recent innovation in drinking water safety. UV light disinfection devices glow with a lethal ultraviolet light that either kills or damages many different species of waterborne troublemakers. These pathogens are either murdered outright by the blast of light, or they are too disabled to breed. In either case, they are no longer a threat. Here are the two primary options when shopping for a UV light purifier for water.

Travel with a UV Pen

Ideal for travelers to carry, UV light pens are pocket-friendly purifiers that usually operate off two small batteries. This device works with just the push of a button, and you can even use it sitting at a restaurant table. Take the cover off the device and stick the light bulb element in your glass of water or your water bottle. Press the button and the light will glow, bombarding any organisms in the water with a 45-second light show. For best results, the water should be clear and the light bulb should be stirred in the water. Typically, clear water (without ice) is safe to drink immediately. If you had any doubt or the water was slightly cloudy, use the device a second or even a third time.

Go Off the Grid with a UV Hand Crank Model

Never worry about the batteries again. In addition to battery powered UV disinfection devices, you can also find hand crank UV purifiers on the market. With a little manual labor, the crank device provides enough power to zap the water with UV light for water disinfection. Start by filling the kit's water bottle from a clear source. Tightly screw the bottle into the housing and turn the entire thing over. Turn the crank until the LED light glows green. Unscrew the bottle from the device (and it's a good idea to wipe the bottle threads clean) and your water is ready. Similarly to a portable UV pen, don't hesitate to "double tap" the water with two doses of light, if the water is slightly cloudy or from a more questionable source.

The Dark Side of UV Light

Like most things, there's a "dark" side to this technique. UV disinfection equipment is only reliable in crystal clear water. If your raw water source is muddy, murky, cloudy, or has significant bits of flotsam bobbing around in it, these particles create hiding places for viruses, bacteria, and other undesirable organisms. These particles may block the light from the UV device, even if multiple doses of UV light are delivered. Only use clear water with this method.

4
Practical Water Storage and Containers

I have a hard time imagining what it was like for our ancestors before they discovered the usefulness of water containers. Only knowing how to hold water by the handful, they must have had many thirsty days, going from one water source to the next. They must have also suffered the loss of loved ones when they were unable to find water several days in a row. As we've discussed, modern people tend to take water for granted, like it will always be there for them. But in the face of an emergency, this may not be the case. Whether lost in the wild or struggling through a disaster, the only guarantee of safe drinking water is to have some stored, and that can only happen when we have containers. From humble beginnings like clay pots to space age plastic bottles, containers can vary greatly but they all do two main jobs: they allow us to store water and they allow us to transport it. Imagine crossing a desert without a canteen or trekking into the mountains without a water bottle. It's not a position you'd want to find yourself in.

Happily, there are plenty of options for water vessels, both commercially available modern containers and the old ways of holding water just like our predecessors used. In this chapter, we'll take a look at the containers you should be carrying and some backup plans should you get caught without them.

Rule Number One—Bring Water!

Remember those thirsty ancestors we talked about? Don't be like them. Bring plenty of water with you into the wild and always keep many jugs of water stored in your home to prepare you for emergencies there. Wishing that you will find water wherever you go, especially in dry environments, can leave you without any water, creating the conditions in which you could die of dehydration. Even when water is indicated on your map, streams may go dry and droughts can hold back the rain. Water is heavy—eight pounds per gallon—and no one wants to carry heavy weights if they can help it. But the thing is, you can't help it. Planning to find all your water along the way is a terrible plan. You're essentially planning to put yourself in a dangerous position. The only water that you are guaranteed to have is the water that you are smart enough to bring along with you.

Contemporary Water Container Options

There are plenty of water containers on the market today, and many are tailored to outdoor settings and home water storage. These are just a few of your options.

Water Bottles

Both metal and plastic water bottles can play an important role in your water storage and transportation plans. I use them both on different occasions and find them to be very valuable. Ordinary plastic water bottles like the ones you'd carry when hiking are lightweight and rugged. For the best durability and versatility, choose bottles that are made from Lexan plastic. Typically, smoky grey in color, these bottles can withstand high temperatures and hold up to many drops and crashes. You can boil water in these bottles by dropping small hot stones inside them—wide mouth bottles work best for this survival hack. Another container option is the metal water bottle. Insulated bottles are great for keeping hot drinks warm and cold drinks cool, but they do limit your "off label" usage. However, single-wall metal bottles commonly made from stainless steel do offer you another option for use beyond just carrying water. Single-wall water bottles can be placed beside a fire for boiling. And don't forget about old-fashioned canteens. You can pick them up at many outdoor stores or Army/Navy surplus stores. Those old green Army canteens may taste and smell a little strange, but they are rugged, light, and ergonomically shaped for comfortable carry. These are also available with canteen covers, to insulate the water and facilitate belt carrying. You can even buy a nesting metal canteen cup that slides over the outside of the canteen for cooking and boiling water.

Hydration Bladders

Another handy container on the market is the hydration bladder. Some of these are simply flexible plastic or rubbery bags that hold water like a soft-sided water bottle. Others, which are often larger, are designed to fit into a backpack and provide drinking water through a convenient drinking hose. Many supportive products are available for hydration bladders and bags. From cleaning accessories to inline water filters, your hydration bladder can be modified to suit your needs.

Make Your Own Water Containers

Our ancestors couldn't get water bottles and hydration bladders at the outdoor sporting goods store, and in certain emergency situations, you won't be able to go shopping either. But don't let that stop you from creating your own containers from available materials. You may even be surprised at the effectiveness of some of these crazy containers.

Make a Bamboo "Bottle"

Bamboo is an oversized grass that has hollow sections in between the joints along its stalks. These alternating solid and hollow sections allow us to cut large bamboo sections to create a variety of vessels. By cutting sections horizontally, you can make single-use cooking containers from green bamboo. You can also cut dead or live bamboo into bottle-shaped sections that act like a canteen.

Clean Out a Gourd

These cultivated plants are found worldwide, and they can be hollowed out and used as lightweight and fairly durable water containers. Just cut off the top of a dried gourd, then scrape away the pithy innards and seeds. For a final step, use sandpaper or a rough stone to sand down the interior of the gourd and fill it up with water. For a more temporary alternative, non-toxic fruit and vegetable rinds can also hold water.

Fold Some Bark

This method of container making is complex and requires some skill, but it is possible to fold a container from flexible non-toxic tree bark. An ancient skill still seen around the world, fresh peeled bark has been and still is used to make buckets and dishes when freshly peeled from suitable trees and carefully folded into water-holding shapes. Think of this as the most unforgiving form of origami on earth.

Use Animal Parts

Though very capable of growing bacteria that could sicken us, rawhide water buckets made from dried animal hide can provide us with a smelly yet durable container. Worse still are organ containers made from fresh or dried stomachs and bladders of large animals. These require removal from the animal, a thorough cleaning process, and they are typically turned inside out. It's an option, but it's best to consider this as last resort and take some steps to disinfect the water after carrying it in a hide or organ vessel.

Stretch a Condom

Shocking, silly, and strangely effective, prophylactics can provide us with one of the most bizarre water containers. The average condom can hold more than one quart of water, but it's tricky to fill. First you need to stretch it to relax the material. Then you'll have to sweep it quickly through the water to expand it like a balloon. Once enough water goes inside, the condom will swell and provide a very strange "water bottle" for carrying water to a new location.

Carry Water in the Form of Ice

This is a little weird, but in sub-freezing or very cold environments, it is possible to carry water without any containers at all. You can simply carry water in its solid form—and that is ice. By locating some freshwater ice along a waterway, breaking off a chunk and tossing it in your backpack, you've found a convenient way to carry water to a new location. We should assume that the water has pathogens frozen in it and that the hypothermia-inducing conditions would make "ice eating" a terrible strategy for hydration. Those problems aside, just chip off some ice, melt it over a fire and then bring it to a boil for safety.

PART II
FIRE

5
The Foundations of Fire Making

Now that you've learned how to effectively find and disinfect drinking water, we'll move on to the second skill set in this book—making fire. Most experts agree that humans first began using fire from sources that were already burning on the landscape. This activity predates the knowledge of how to make fire from scratch, and we likely collected these wildfires for a much longer period of time than we have been creating fire from raw materials that were not burning on their own. These "found" fires were likely the result of lightning strikes in dry areas and minor lava flows, both of which could ignite dead, dry vegetation and provide our ancestors with their first experience of fire. I'm sure that our predecessors were frightened of fire at first, feeling the same instinctive fear that animals still exhibit. But over time, fear turned to curiosity and we began to "play" with fire. Learning how to feed a fire, how to maintain it, and how to transport it from place to place—these were major and pivotal developments in human history. To this very day, those same skills can be game-changing assets in the wilderness. You don't even need to be in a predicament to take advantage of the benefits of fire. This glowing element provides us with both necessities and comforts in the wild. It gives us warmth and light during conditions that are cold and dark. It also transforms materials, like raw meat and dirty water—changing them into cooked food and a safe beverage. Fire does many other tasks as well, but in order to take advantage of all the things that fire can do, we'll have to learn about the fuels necessary to create fire and how to keep that fire burning safely and effectively even in weather that would extinguish its friendly, warm glow.

Understanding Fire

What is fire? We can certainly explain it in scientific terms. Fire is the rapid oxidation of materials through the process of combustion. In other words, if you have burnable materials that get hot enough in the presence of oxygen, you'll get fire as the result. But is fire more than just the release of heat, light, gasses, smoke, and ash? From a more philosophical approach, fire is a tool, a companion, and a destroyer. It's even been called a "pet," since we end up feeding it, cleaning up after it, and trying to tame it. To really understand fire, we must gain experience in balancing three vital resources—heat, fuel, and oxygen. Often referred to as the fire triangle (or combustion triangle), this basic trifecta reminds us of the necessary components that allow fire to exist and to continue.

Heat

The heat to initiate combustion can come from many different sources. For our purposes as fire makers, the heat will be our "ignition method"—the manner in which we start the fire. Heat can come from matches, lighters, spark rods, magnifying glasses, wood friction, exothermic chemical reactions, electricity, and pressure (just to name a few).

Fuel

This is the material we are burning. Many materials can be broken down with high heat, but in our case we will use materials that are readily available, easy to ignite, and capable of sustaining a fire. Dead dry plant materials fit our needs quite well, though many different things can be burned as fuel. For fire making ease, fuels are usually divided into three categories—tinder, kindling, and firewood. Once the fuel is burning, it releases heat, light, and various gasses. Once it has burnt, the fuel becomes ash. This is the non-combustible residue left over from a fire, mainly consisting of oxides and carbonates of potassium, magnesium, and calcium depending on the fuel that was burnt.

Oxygen

This fire component is usually free for the taking. Earth's atmosphere is almost 21 percent oxygen and unless a fire is snuffed out somehow, your fire should have all the oxygen it needs.

How Does Blowing on a Fire Help?

When a new fire is just getting started with a tiny volume of embers and little flames, it's easy to blow it out—just like you'd blow out a candle. Once your fire has grown a base of embers that are at least the size of golf balls, an interesting change occurs. With a heat base established, a sluggish fire can be blown on or fanned with any reasonable flat object

(continued next page)

to help it to burn better. Several things are happening when you fan or blow on a struggling fire. You're removing ash, which blocks the gas exchange needed for combustion. More importantly, you're also moving more oxygen through the area where the reaction is occurring. Remember the heat, fuel, and oxygen trifecta. By adding the right thing at the right time, you'll find fire starting to be a much easier task.

Tinder

When you are trying to build a fire, the very first fuel you feed it is a critical choice. I often explain it to my survival classes as "baby food" for their infant fire. This first fuel is called tinder, and this is typically some kind of fluffy plant-based material that is dead and dry. A good tinder material will be able to turn an ember or a tiny flame into a fire that can produce enough heat to burn kindling and eventually, firewood. The kind of tinder you'll want to use will have three main things in common. First, the fuel must be dry. The perfect tinder material can be processed to its optimum texture, and it still won't burn if it's too wet or too green (still alive). Dryness is the key to your success. Second, your tinder choice must come from the plant kingdom. These materials should be dead, but not too rotten. Decomposed plant materials usually have a lower fuel value, and they do not burn as well as materials that are dead without being rotten. Our third and final condition is that the tinder material should be fluffy. Without a lot of surface area, the tinder won't have the best fuel-to-air ratio for lighting that baby fire. You may have to scrape it, pound it, shred it, or crumble it to reach this optimal texture but it helps the materials to reach their combustion temperature quickly—and it's worth any trouble you have to endure. What follows is a list of six very common tinder materials and the ignition methods that work best for each one.

Left to right, leaves, grass, pine needles, bark fiber, weed tops, and wood shavings.

Leaves

Some people don't like using dead leaves as tinder, but I happen to like these cast-off parts from trees and plants. Some tree species even hold onto their dead leaves through the winter, providing sun-dried tinder day and night. Collect your dead leaves away from the ground or in sunny, protected areas. Avoid the leaves on the ground or in damp areas, as these will contain more moisture. Most leaves will crumble into small flakes when dead and fully dried, so this can be your test of general quality (prior to an actual burn test). Leaves light best with an open flame, though they can be crumbled into a ball and hit with the sparks from a spark rod or lit with a magnifying glass.

Grasses

Although most grass tinder is heavily impacted by moisture, dead grass blades and stems can be used as single-species tinder or blended with other materials. Grass can burn furiously in dry conditions, though it may not burn at all when damp. Use an open flame to light any dead grass parts. For spark rod fire starting, collect finer dead leaf blades and fluffy seed tops. Odd fact: grass tinder needs to have died on its own and turned yellow, tan, or grey. Grass that is cut green and then dried, like lawn trimmings and hay, retains significant amounts of nitrogen and moisture, both of which will put out fires.

Evergreen Needles

The dead brown needles from evergreen trees can be used as a long-burning tinder and they offer some resistance to dampness. These generally light best with an open flame, though fine, slender needles may be able to light with other ignition methods.

Inner Tree Bark

The fibrous dead inner bark from certain trees (and even the outer bark layer of a few species) can be peeled and processed to become fire-starting tinder. I often use the inner bark from dead branches of tulip poplar, pawpaw, and certain oaks on the Central East Coast of the United States. The outer bark of cypress, cedar, juniper, and other trees can also be stripped from live or dead wood. Each of these can be processed into great tinder by shredding or pounding and then ignited with either sparks or flames.

Weed Tops

The highly variable group of weed tops usually involves the dead seed tops from assorted plants. These tops may consist of nothing but fluffy material, such as cattail seed heads. These can catch the sparks from spark rods, though as a fuel, cattail seed head fluff tends to just smolder rather than stay aflame. Other weed tops may contain several different grades of tinder material, which include fluffy seed down, papery chaff, and tiny twigs. These mixed-fuel weed tops can burn well, igniting from either flames or sparks. Common seed down choices include thistle, dogbane, cattail, milkweed, and goldenrod. The dead flower heads of many other plants can also be used as a coarser grade of tinder. When using these materials, I prefer to place weed tops and seed down as a central core for tinder bundles or mix them into more fibrous materials rather than using them as a stand-alone fuel.

Cattail seed down is one of the best and most common weed tops for tinder.

Wood Shavings

If you have wood to burn, you have wood that can be scraped or carved into wood shavings—a tinder source that comes straight from the firewood. It might even be your best bet in perpetually wet areas. Cut the wet bark and damp outer layer of wood off your firewood, then use a sharp-edged tool to make shavings from the drier wood below. This can be done on both hardwood and softwood species, and even dead bamboo stalks can yield fluffy scraped tinder. In the event that the tools or the materials won't yield fine shavings, use a sharp edge to carve off coarse shavings. These won't be likely to light from a spark rod, though they should light from an open flame. Wood shaving tinder is the most laborious tinder to create, but in certain conditions, it's your only choice.

Tinder to Avoid

Some fluffy materials are perfect for fire starting but fluffiness is no guarantee of flammability. Useful tinder typically comes from the plant kingdom. Fluffy things from the animal kingdom may look like good tinder materials, but most are not suitable. Hair, fur, feathers, wool, and leather scraps will burn when you throw them into a wood fire, but they do not burn well on their own (a key trait of tinder). Animal fibers and hairs just melt, shrivel, and stink. Unless they are both dry and oily, they won't catch flame and continue to burn. For best results, stick to the plant kingdom as the raw source for all of your tinder materials.

Kindling

This is the intermediate fuel in fire building, which bridges the gap between tinder and firewood. In most areas, if you've got wood to burn, you'll likely have twigs and sticks for kindling, though this isn't always the case. These slender woody materials are easy to grab and effective to use but they aren't the only form of kindling you can use.

Sticks. Dead dry sticks, twigs, and branches are one of the most common kindling materials around the globe. You'll want the sticks that are still attached to the tree or shrub, and for most woody plant species they will snap off when dead and dry. Avoid sticks and branches with any green growth as these are still alive and full of moisture.

Plant Stalks. Dead weeds, grass stalks, and similar vegetation can be used as quick-burning kindling. In arid climates, these stalks and stems can be abundant and explosively flammable. In wetter areas, use the upper portion of dead stalks, since the lower part will be damper.

Split Kindling. If you have wood to burn, you can split that wood down into kindling sticks with a knife or hatchet. In the aftermath of storms you can also find broken branches and tree trunks that yield "ready-made" wood-splinter kindling.

Flammable Bark. Most outer tree barks are corky materials that are in place to protect the tree from a fire (not to help them burn to the ground). However, a few tree species do happen to have outer bark that can act like kindling. Several birch species have an oily outer layer of bark that peels off in horizontal strips from the trunk and larger branches. This can be peeled and ignited with an open flame to act as a twig alternative or supplement. Birch bark even burns when wet thanks to its high oil content.

Hazardous Kindling. Not every twig wants to be your friend. The dead branches and vines from poison ivy, poison oak, and other toxic woody plants can be harmful when handled and they become very dangerous when burned. Take the time to learn about your local hazardous plant species and learn how to avoid grabbing their dead growth for fire materials. Even something as mild as poison ivy can become a serious hazard when burned, since the damaging oils can be transported by the fire's smoke.

Unconventional Kindling. Snack chips are a common food that many hikers and campers carry for nourishment in the wild. Most of these high fat treats are also very flammable. With the open flame provided by a match or lighter, oily chips can burn with high heat and they can even light damp fire lays. Try burning some on your next camping trip.

Most people are surprised to see their favorite snack going up in flames.

Firewood

Once the tinder has done its job of igniting the kindling, it's time to include the third stage of fuel, which is firewood. These are the larger pieces of woody material that are capable of burning for longer periods of time. Some camping locations require visitors to only collect "dead fall" firewood, which are the dead limbs and branches that are lying on the ground. In a wilderness setting without such rules, you'll be much better off breaking down limbs and branches from standing dead woody plants like trees and shrubs. The standing dead wood will be much drier and less likely to be rotten. With simple tools like saws and axes, firewood can be cut and split quickly and easily. Without these tools, you may need to rely on smaller materials that can be broken by hand. Once your fire is large enough to consume big firewood pieces, you should be able to maintain it indefinitely as long as the fuel keeps coming and rain doesn't put it out.

"Cutting" Firewood Without Tools

If you're looking for a way to reduce long logs and branches into short firewood pieces without saws or axes, there are actually two simple techniques you can use. The first is to burn the wood into shorter lengths with your campfire and the other technique is to break the wood with leverage. Burning the wood into sections is as easy as it sounds. Throw a longer branch or log over the fire and allow the flames to burn it into two pieces. If long enough, these could be separated into further pieces. As for breaking the wood with leverage, that technique is as simple as placing the branch in a rock crevice or between two trees and pushing on the end of the branch. If the branch isn't too thick or strong, it should break at the fulcrum point (where it is in contact with the restraining object). Now you're working smarter, instead of working harder.

Safe Fire Locations

Now that you have a better understanding of the fuels needed for fire building, it's important to plan a safe and practical place for the fire to burn. Since our earliest days of fire usage, the hearth that holds the fire has been a central point in camps and villages. Sure, you could build and use a fire in any spot, but your fire will serve you best if you take the time to pick a good location before you light it.

Overhead Hazards. Even though it seems like a sheltered location, you'll want to avoid building a fire underneath low branches on evergreen trees—especially dead evergreen branches, which are very flammable. It's also a bad idea to build under snowy evergreen limbs and boughs. The rising heat will melt the snow and drop it directly on top of your fire. Finally, you'll never want stone overhead in your fire area. Using caves and rock overhangs as a fire location will heat up the rock, causing it to expand and crack. This could lead to rocks falling on you. I can hear the arguments building now. "Well, didn't the cavemen have fires in their caves?" Yeah, certainly, but they were also simpletons.

Keep Your Distance. Never build your fire near flammable plant materials like dead grassy fields, dried brush, or drought-stricken pine lands. You'll even want to rake away ground debris and leaves from your fire area, creating a ten-foot circle where nothing can ignite other than your fire. You'll also want to avoid building your fire up against fallen tree trunks, rotten stumps, and standing dead trees. These materials can ignite and smolder for days, creating a wildfire long after you've moved on. As a final consideration for fire location, you'll want to burn your fire at least ten feet away from your shelter, especially if it's a survival shelter made from flammable plant material. You'll also want the fire to be downwind from your shelter. Since sparks can drift on a breeze and leafy survival shelters can catch fire from a spark, the prevailing winds should blow from the shelter toward the fire and not the other way around.

Fire Lays

Prowl the internet and you'll find dozens of different fuel configurations that are described as fire lays. Some may share structural similarities or similar fuels, while others are wildly different. Each of these fire-starting structures also seems to have loyal followers who don't want to use any other structure. Regardless of their architecture, these fire lays all share some basic features. They are relatively small structures, constructed from tinder and kindling. Their sole purpose is to establish a fire and create enough heat to ignite larger materials, namely firewood. After you gain some experience, you may find that you have a preferred fire lay for different occasions. Here are just a few of the most typical and useful fire lay styles.

Log Cabin Fire

A lot of folks like the log cabin fire lay. It can take a little time to build, but it's stable and it burns well. Start by building a square stick "fence" with a tinder pile in the center. It can be any size, though something around eight or ten inches across is good for a small one. A little over one foot across is a good size for a larger log cabin. Once the walls are built up, use more sticks to build a tipi inside the walls (your best bet) or lay the sticks overtop the wall. It's like creating a roof, though it's not as effective. This configuration is dependable and long burning though it's the longest to build and takes up the most material.

Tipi Fire

This setup is my favorite and I use it the most. Simply build a cone of sticks with a large wad of tinder in the middle. Use thinner and finer twigs right next to the tinder and use increasingly thicker twigs and kindling as you reach the outer section of the cone-shaped wall. The tipi shape should have a matching height-to-base width for optimum results. For example, a cone of sticks that is one foot tall should have a base that is one foot wide. Because of the outstanding "fuel to air" mixture, the tipi fire lay is easy to light and reliable. This structure can be assembled one stick at a time building upon a ball of tinder in the center, or you can build it as you collect the materials. Gather your twigs and kindling sticks in one hand, placing the thicker end of each twig in your hand. This naturally creates a cone shape, which can then be stuffed with tinder in the center. Break off any long twigs so that the wider end of the cone is flat and place the flat end on the ground. Wiggle the structure until it feels stable, and you should have a free-standing cone that takes very little time to build.

Stable and efficient, the tipi fire lay is a classic.

V-Wall Fire

This one is often used to focus the wind into the fire lay for more effective burning. Start by crossing two sticks to make a 90-degree V-shaped form where you plan to build your fire. Make sure the V opens into the wind so that it acts like a natural funnel to collect and direct the airflow. Continue stacking kindling in an overlapping pattern, building an angular wall about six inches tall. Place a bundle or pile of tinder material at the inside bend of the wall, then rest a few sticks across the tinder (similar to a tipi structure). Light the structure when ready.

Lean-To Fire

If you're looking for a quick fire lay in favorable fire conditions, try the lean-to fire lay. It's easy to build and frugal on materials. To build it, just take a thicker piece of your firewood and lay it in your fireplace. Set a generous tinder pile next to the wood and lay a "lean-to wall" of kindling overtop the tinder. That's it. Light it up and you're on your way to building a campfire.

This fast fire lay allows good air flow and only requires minimal kindling.

Tips for Lighting Any Fire Lay

Whichever fire lay you build, you'll have better luck lighting any of them with these simple tips.

Light It Low. Most people fail in fire making because they try to light the top of a fire lay as if it were a candle. This is fundamentally wrong, since heat rises and fire climbs. Instead, light the fire lay as close to the ground as possible, so that the fire can quickly climb through the pile of materials above your ignition spot.

Use the Wind. While a strong wind can blow out your matches and push away the heat of a fledgling fire, a light breeze can fan the flames with no effort on your part. In addition to lighting the fire low on the fire lay, light the fire lay on the side that the breeze is coming from. This can push the heat into your structure, rather than having the heat blow out the open side of the structure and be lost to the air flow.

Stay Still. I see many beginners moving their matches around as if they are in some frantic race to light as many spots on the fire lay as possible before their fingertips get burnt. You'd be better served to pick a spot low on the structure on the upwind side and hold your match in place until you can't hold it anymore. This concentrates more heat in one spot and offers you a better chance of success. Don't believe me? Try both techniques and see which one is more reliable, in all kinds of weather and with all different materials.

Common Mistakes with Fire Lays

Beginners often make the same mistakes and even more seasoned outdoor enthusiasts can make the same blunders from time to time. Keep an eye out for these frequent failures and you'll be way ahead of the game.

Don't Build a Hollow House. When making a fire lay, it's as if you're making a little house for your fire to dwell in. But unlike a house, there shouldn't be any significant voids inside the structure. Materials need to be touching or nearly touching for fire to transfer from one item to the next. Pack the fire lay tightly with tinder and slender twigs and don't worry about building a structure that's too dense. If there's a void inside the fire lay, you'll find that the core of your fire lay burns up without spreading the fire to the outer materials.

Avoid Green Branches. Especially in winter, it's hard to tell which twigs and branches are alive and which ones are dead. You'll only want the dead ones for kindling, since the live ones have too much moisture to burn effectively. If deciduous twigs seem too flexible, have heathy buds on the twig tips, or have any little piece of greenery on them, don't collect them. In sub-freezing weather, you can also try a "feel test." When twigs are alive, they have high moisture levels. When touched to your warm bare skin, these live twigs will feel extra cold. Because of the lack of moisture in dead twigs, they will warm up quickly against your skin and feel very different to live twigs. Just be careful of this technique in frostbite weather, since exposed skin is in jeopardy.

Don't Collect from the Ground. I see it all the time in my classes. Students grab sticks off the ground for kindling, not realizing how much more moisture they contain than dead twigs still on the trees and bushes. The ground has its own moisture and it's the place where precipitation collects. Grab your kindling up high and make sure it's dead for best results.

6
Modern Fire-Starting Methods

With a good working knowledge of fire-starting fuels and safe places to build a fire, now you're ready to delve into our first round of ignition methods—modern fire-starting equipment. And while these fire-igniting methods aren't exactly cutting-edge technology (in fact, some of them are over a century old), these pieces of equipment are light years ahead of "rubbing two sticks together" for fire. In this chapter, we'll take an in-depth look at some of the most practical and readily available fire-starting tools that are at our disposal today. We'll also explore some of the weirder fire-lighting methods that are available to the modern outdoor enthusiast and survival skills practitioner. The first two starting methods in this chapter are the tools that we should always have at our side, in our wilderness survival kits, and in our emergency response gear. The other two methods are odd and unusual, yet still valid as ignition methods. These latter methods are best explained as survival hacks, suitable in a time and place where our normal supplies are spent or out of reach. Together, these four methods are some of the easiest ways to build your own fire, and no doubt, they'd have our ancestors turning green with envy. Before we begin, I'd like to share one word of warning. Even though the following four methods can get you a fire with relative ease, there is a learning curve to all new skills. Don't just read about the methods. Try them out and test your skills. Although I say that something is easier than something else, you should still judge for yourself. Also keep in mind that ease of use isn't the only factor in fire starting. The easiest and most effective fire starter on the planet still won't get you a fire if your materials are terrible or the weather conditions are too harsh (i.e. it's raining buckets).

Lighters

Pocket-sized lighters that are largely used for lighting cigarettes are a common sight today and they are one of our easiest fire starters to use. They provide us with an open flame, and they can be operated by just one hand which is a major benefit in the wake of an injury, like a broken arm. Originally developed over a hundred years ago, naphtha-filled lighters like the Austrian IMCO cigarette lighter, the Ronson "Wonderlite" and the later Zippo lighter all shared similar traits. They acted like a refillable portable candle, using a liquid fuel-soaked wick that lit from a small ferrocerium rod. With the development of plastics a few decades later, the disposable butane lighter gained traction in the early 1970s and has become the most common style of lighter today. As a survival tool, they are a great choice—readily available and very effective. With just one working thumb and the lighter, you can create a small flame with push-button ease. Here are some of the particulars of naphtha and butane lighters.

Naphtha Lighters. These are reusable lighters that are filled with a liquid naphtha product, commonly lighter fluid. These allow one-handed lighting similar to other types of lighters, but they offer a unique feature—hands-free operation. Once lit, there's no need to hold down a button. Light the device and set it down to act as a light source, just like a candle. This all sounds great but there is one major flaw. Naphtha evaporates over time and unless you carry a small bottle of lighter fluid, you may find yourself out of fuel at the worst possible time. There is one bright side, however, to this fleeting fuel source. It almost forces you to carry a small bottle of lighter fluid, which could save the day when attempting to make fire in harsh conditions. If you decide against carrying extra fuel, just make sure the reservoir is full before each outing. You might also want to learn how to make a fire from the tiny ferrocerium "flint" on the lighter. Both an empty Zippo and an empty butane lighter are still capable of making fire when they are out of fuel. Insert a tiny tuft of fluffy tinder, or better yet, a bit of char cloth, which we will discuss in Chapter 7, into the sparking area of the lighter and strike the wheel until the tinder lights. Immediately move the tuft into a larger tinder bundle to catch the quick burning tuft of tinder. Blow the tinder into flame, as you would with any other ember-based ignition method and enjoy your fire from an empty lighter.

Butane Lighters. The various brands of butane lighters will have some different features and qualities, but most are very affordable and trustworthy. Simpler models, like Bic lighters, offer rugged construction and few moving parts. Other companies offer additional features, like an adjustable flame height. Adjustable flames can be useful in an emergency as you can burn a smaller than normal flame to be frugal on fuel in a long-term emergency. You can also dial the flame up taller for extra assistance in windy or wet weather fire making. Just keep in mind that more moving parts mean that there are more parts to break and I've found these adjustable lighters to be less durable. Of course, we wouldn't want our gear to break during a survival situation, but there is a work around for a damaged lighter. If the fuel cartridge and button are still intact but the spark wheel is broken or missing, you can still get a flame from your lighter. If you're with your survival buddy, have them hold down the button on the lighter as you strike sparks from another ferrocerium rod. When these are near the butane outlet, you'll have flame again. And if you're out there solo, try a bit of tape to hold down the button, then strike the sparks yourself—aiming at the lighter mouth. Use the lighter as needed, then peel off the tape to release the button.

Tips for Lighter Use

Butane lighters will give you fire at the push of a button, but that doesn't mean they are flawless. In temperatures below freezing, the liquid butane inside the lighter will start to change forms—shifting from a flowing liquid into a gelatinous ooze. Since it needs to be in liquid form for the lighter to work, we'll need to warm the lighter so the gel turns back into liquid. Just hold it in your warm hand for a minute or two, and it should perform normally again. Better yet, carry it inside your coat or in a pants pocket so that it never gets cold in the first place.

Don't Mind the Moisture

If your butane lighter takes a swim, don't worry—it's not ruined. The sealed fuel cartridge is waterproof, and the ferrocerium striker is immune to water as well. If your lighter gets wet for any reason, just shake out any drops of water

(continued next page)

you see or try blowing on the spark wheel, then strike the lighter as you normally would. Naphtha-fueled lighters will have a little more trouble after a dunking and these are best revitalized by taking them apart and drying them completely before refilling them with fresh fuel.

Ferrocerium Rods

Often misidentified in modern survival shows and literature as "flint," ferrocerium was originally known as Auermetall in Europe (named after its Austrian inventor, Baron Carl Auer von Welsbach). The Baron's first attempt to create a fire-starting substance in 1903 involved blending iron and cerium. It's from this combination that we derive the name ferrocerium (ferro meaning "iron," from the Latin word *ferrum*).

This waterproof tool creates hot sparks that can quickly ignite fluffy tinder.

Later alloys saw the addition of lanthanum and other rare-earth minerals for bigger sparks and greater durability. Today, the typical ferrocerium rod (also called a firesteel) has a composition of roughly 42 percent cerium, 24 percent lanthanum, 20 percent iron, and equal amounts of praseodymium, neodymium, and magnesium. This material is usually formed into rods, which are then coated with hardening compounds like iron oxide and magnesium oxide (the black exterior of the rods). This black coating must be scraped away before the rod will be able to make a fire, though this is easily done with the same sharp edge you'll use to make sparks for fire starting. Once the rod is free of its coating, the hot sparks that fly from it can exceed temperatures of 3,000°C (5,430°F). This is due to the rapid oxidization of the scraped rod fragments as they are heated from the friction of scraping and exposed to the oxygen in the air. This material is used for the flint in most cigarette lighters and it works as a durable fire starter—even in intense cold and wet conditions.

Choose Your Tinder Carefully

With ferrocerium rods, your best approach for success is to use fluffy natural plant materials for your tinder. Some things that would normally light with an open flame (like dead leaves) will not easily light with sparks. The short-lived sparks tend to bounce off the hard surfaces rather than nestling in and burning. When you select fibrous and fluffy plant ingredients, the sparks will "stick" better in the fuel and begin to burn. Finely shredded inner bark and airy seed down are some of your best choices for tinder when using spark rods. Some materials from home will also work, like cotton balls and dryer lint from all-cotton loads of laundry. Carry these fuels with your fire-starting kit stored in water-tight containers to virtually guarantee your luck in fire starting.

Don't Move the Scraper—Move the Rod

It's only natural that we would want to move the scraping tool to make shavings, but there's a problem with this when we are throwing sparks into tinder. By moving the scraper forward and toward the tinder, we often hit the tinder with the scraper and knock it apart. The solution to this problem is simple, and it just involves a change of technique. Rather than moving the scraper forward, hold the scraper stationary and pull the rod backward (as if you're pulling the cord to start a lawnmower). This drives a shower of intensely hot sparks right into the tinder, without the destructive scraper stroke.

Make the Most of Magnesium

Often sold alongside other fire starters, the magnesium bar fire starter is a block of soft grey metal with a ferrocerium rod glued to its side. The purpose of this partnership is to provide both an ignition source (the rod) and a fuel source (the magnesium). The kit usually includes a small steel scraper for use on the rod and the bar. To use the set as intended, use the provided tool to scrape off tiny shavings of magnesium (ideally, scraping them into a container). You could also scrape the magnesium bar with the square spine of your knife or the blade if you have to, but this will dull it significantly. Once you have enough metal shavings to cover a coin, pour them into a tight tinder bundle and strike ferrocerium sparks into the magnesium shavings. Be careful not to jostle the tinder, as it will spread out the metal shavings. These grey slivers burn best when they are clumped into a pile and finely shaved. Once lit, the magnesium will burn white hot for a second or two, hopefully igniting your tinder. It's also worth knowing that you could skip the magnesium shaving and hold the grey block as a handle. A quality tinder bundle should ignite from the ferrocerium sparks alone. The biggest pros for this kit are affordability and toughness.

The biggest con is the fact that the glue can break and the rod can be lost.

Fire by Electricity

The contemporary do-it-yourself crowd and generations of tradesmen are very familiar with steel wool, as it excels at cleaning metal and sanding wood, but few people are aware of the flammable nature of this odd material. Even though you won't find steel wool in the wild, for those who have this multi-use material and the right battery, you can quickly make a fire when bringing together the right combination. You'll find this supply in hardware stores and some craft suppliers. Look for "fine" grade steel wool (more zeros on the label are better) and find a battery that's at least 3-volts. You'll want a battery that has the positive and negative terminals near each other. 9-volt and 6-volt batteries are a great choice, due to voltage and terminal placement. You can also make other batteries work, by joining them together in a way that makes a circuit with at least 3-volts and terminals close together. To make your fire from these unexpected items, simply touch a small wad of steel wool to both terminals at the same time. The steel wool will begin to burn, and it can be placed into tinder to be blown into flame.

Make Fire with a Car Battery

If you don't have any steel wool, don't let that stop you from building a fire using electricity as an ignition method. The very same car battery that can start your vehicle can also start a fire. This method is riskier than the others in this book as the vehicle battery can explode. Only use this method if you have no other options and your car lacks a cigarette lighter (many older cars have these, while very few new cars do). To make a car battery fire, connect your jumper cables to the positive and negative terminals of the battery. When ready, take the free ends of the cables and touch the inner part of the metal jaws to each other. Do this in a quick sweeping motion, directly over a dry tinder bundle. Do not clamp the jaws together. These must only touch for a second and separate. If you're not careful, the jaws will weld together and create a closed circuit with the battery. This can cause the battery to overheat, which could cause a dangerous and acidic explosion. Wear eye protection and gloves when performing this method. And for those who are more timid (or perhaps wiser), you can also make a fire with the battery, jumper cables, and a two-inch section of a wooden pencil that has been sharpened on both ends. Clamp the jumper cable jaws to the exposed graphite on each end of the pencil and it will burst into flame in just a moment.

Create Fire with Chemicals

This is the least common of the "modern" fire-starting methods, and frankly, it's the least reliable method, too. I've had it work many times, and I've had it fail many times. The typical chemicals involved are potassium permanganate and glycerin. Several decades ago, the US military would include small bottles of dark purple potassium permanganate crystals in first aid kits and other gear. The odd granular powder can be applied on wounds to prevent infection. This substance can also be added to raw water sources to disinfect the water. The recipe is easy enough. Add enough powder for a significant color change, and "when it's pink, safe to drink." The strangest use, however, has always been as a fire starter. To try it, pour out a small pile of potassium permanganate crystals on the surface you intend to start a fire. Use your fingertip to place a little dent in the middle of the pile, so that it looks like a little crater. Drip several drops of glycerin into the crater and wait for the reaction to take place. If the ratios are right, the chemicals will begin to bubble and then quickly burn like a road flare. Add tinder on top of the burning chemicals and then add kindling to continue building the fire. There is one other option, which is even less reliable but interesting, and that is to combine friction, potassium permanganate crystals, and granulated table sugar. Blend a little of each powder on a flat dry surface (like a rock or the inside of a bark slab). Grind the powders together aggressively with a blunt stick. Add the tinder when you see a tint of combustion and keep grinding. This is less likely to work than using glycerin, and it is less likely to work than any other "modern" method, but you still have a chance of success.

7
Historic Fire-Making Techniques

Just because something is old it doesn't necessarily mean that it's outdated or ineffective. Take the wheel, as an example. This rolling invention dates back at least 5,000 years, and there's still no better shape for the tires on your car than a round wheel. New technology can be very important and we often assume that "newer equals better," but keep in mind that there are many things from the past that are worth carrying forward into the future. When it comes to fire, I recommend that you always carry modern fire-starting equipment like butane lighters and spark rods in your survival kit just because of their ease of use. However, I also recommend that you take a good hard look at the methods of the past and consider learning about them as a backup plan for emergency fire building. With practice and in the right conditions, the old-fashioned fire-lighting methods in this chapter will be just as effective at kindling a blaze as the modern methods of fire lighting. For this chapter, we'll look at matches, optical fire starting, and the ancient method of flint and steel. Except for matches, these fire-building techniques are sustainable in the field—a trait which could be invaluable in a long-term survival setting. As long as the sun keeps shining and you don't lose your optics, lighting fires with a magnifying lens and parabolic mirror will always be possible. And if you're able to make more charred tinder and find some hard stones, a flint and steel set can work day or night and last for several lifetimes if you don't lose the steel striker in the woods. Yes, there's a learning curve with some of these fire-lighting methods (like scraping more of your knuckles than the steel with flint and steel), but you may also find that you really like some of them.

Flint and Steel

Between the ages of friction fire and matches, one fire-starting method reigned supreme. It was "flint and steel" fire lighting, it was seen all over the globe, and it's one of my favorite methods in this book. I really enjoy making the kits in little metal boxes and stocking them with the best materials I can find. In recent years, I've even started making my own steel strikers from high carbon scrap steel like the leaf springs from junk cars. But even though making my own strikers is something new to me, this method certainly isn't new to the world. The flint and steel fire-making method dates back to the earliest part of the Iron Age in Asia and Europe, while its roots date back even farther into prehistory. Percussive fire lighting with iron pyrites and other natural stones may be tens of thousands of years old, being used throughout the middle and late Stone Age. Whatever its origin may be, percussive fire-starting methods create a red-hot spark by striking the right material against a harder stone edge. This tiny bit of metal or raw ore is heated to a melting point by the pressure and friction of the strike and if you're skillful, you can catch it with exceedingly good tinder such as charred plant fibers. Typically, this striker is a piece of high carbon steel that has been hardened, and it is struck against the edge of a stone that is even harder than the steel. This is usually a flint flake, hence the name flint and steel. The sparks that are produced are much smaller, cooler, and shorter lived than ferrocerium sparks, and this requires us to catch the sparks in a tinder with a very low ignition temperature such as charred cotton cloth. Once the charred material is smoldering and ideally sitting in a good tinder nest, it can be blown into flame. What follows are the items and techniques you'll need to successfully make fire like the ancient ones.

Flint and steel is an old-fashioned fire-starting method that is too good to ignore.

The Striker. This is the piece of steel that is the source material for the fire-starting sparks. Typically formed and hardened by a blacksmith, the striker is the piece you will hit with the edge of a hard sharp stone. Over the centuries and across the world, various cultures have formed steel strikers into different shapes. Today, we see some of the most recent patterns still available. Strikers shaped like the letters "C," capital "D," and lowercase "n" are commonly available from contemporary companies that provide reenactment supplies. Less commonly, you'll see "v"-shaped strikers, simple bar shapes, horseshoe shapes, and even strikers that are attached to straps or pouches. For those who don't mind experimenting, purpose-built strikers aren't the only pieces of metal that will spark when struck by a flint edge. Very old knives may have the right hardness and carbon content to act as an effective striker. Contemporary metal files, the spines of machetes, and parts of other tools may also have the right combination of carbon and hardness to strike sparks. You'll just have to try them and see.

The Stone. Many beginners get hung up when it comes to the rock that they'll need for flint and steel. It doesn't have to be actual flint and it's not a piece of rock that is burning—it's the steel. Your "flint" can be many different types of stone. It just needs an edge that is 90 degrees or sharper and it should be as hard (or harder) than the steel you intend to strike. Ideally, it should be a sharp flat flake of broken rock that is easy to hold but even chunky cube-like pieces will work. Of course, it can be flint stone, but it could also be a chunk of chert, jasper, agate, or granite. In my home area, I routinely use quartz and quartzite. These are very common stones that are more than hard enough for the task. If you find yourself in an area of rounded pebbles and cobbles, just crack one in half by striking it between two stones. You'll get plenty of edges that are sharp enough to spark.

The Charred Material. This is nothing short of the "secret sauce" for the flint and steel technique. Often called "char cloth," this material doesn't have to be a woven textile. In its simplest form, your char is some kind of carefully burnt material that is originally from the plant kingdom. My local favorites for charring are dead and dry cattail plant seed down and finely pounded dead inner bark from the tulip poplar tree. Once charred, these are excellent at catching and feeding the tiny sparks that are shaved off a steel striker. Going back into history, little scraps of old cotton and linen cloth were common materials. Using something more modern, ordinary cotton balls can make a good charred material too. In fact, many of the materials that would make a good fire-starting tinder can also make a good char and even a few materials that won't act as tinder can work. For example, crumbly rotten wood isn't suitable as tinder, but it can be burned to become effective char. Often called "punk wood," this material may be so common and plentiful that it can't be ignored. Other odd char candidates include certain dead fungi, like horse hoof fungus, cracked cap polypore, and chaga. Some of these materials, like chaga fungus, have a low enough ignition temperature that they can simply be ground into a powder and there is no need to char them. Most, however, need to be burned in a low-oxygen environment. Once this is done, the ignition temperature of the char will be between 650°F and 850°F (343°C and 454°C), depending on the raw material and the quality of the charring process. This is typically done by packing favorable raw materials into a small metal container. Candy tins are commonly used for this. They should be nearly airtight but allow some gases to escape during the burning. Rectangular candy tins with a hinged lid will provide enough airflow at the hinge holes. More solid tins, like shoe polish cans, can be pierced once with a nail or the tip of a knife blade to allow airflow. Once your can is prepared, filled with prospective char material and sealed, toss it into the center of a medium-sized fire and allow it to "bake" for five minutes. During this time, smoke should jet from the hole (or holes) in the container, and it may even become a little jet of flame. This will cease after a few minutes and once you've hit the five-minute mark, roll or flip the hot container out of the fire. If possible, I like to cover the hole in the container, to prevent oxygen from getting in while the char is still hot. Once the container is cool to the touch, it can be opened for inspection and testing. The char material should be black, very brittle, and it should have shrunken slightly. Test it by striking sparks against it. If sparks catch and begin to spread across the char, you did everything right. And never worry about your char being "fresh" or "stale." Once you've carbonized the material, it will last indefinitely. Keep your char dry and intact by storing it in the can in which it was burned or keep it in some other waterproof container with your fire-starting gear.

Making Char Without the Metal Container

Don't worry, you're not out of the game if you don't have a metal container to cook your char cloth. Many people experiment with chunks of charcoal from a campfire, but unfortunately, these won't work. They still have fuel value and will reignite when thrown into another fire, but that kind of charcoal was made from dense wood with abundant oxygen in the vicinity. It will not ignite or behave like true char cloth. You can, however, make your own charred material for flint and steel by burning some quality tinder and then snuffing it out to extinguish the flames. If you have a thick glass jar with a lid, ignite your tinder however you can, then drop it into the jar and close the lid. Leave it for a few minutes, and you'll have tinder that is partially raw, partially burnt, and slightly charred. Strike sparks at the charred part, then blow them through the rest of the fuel to get your fire back. And for those caught without a jar, light the tinder and get it burning completely, then squash the tinder bundle on the ground with a flat rock. Leave the rock in place for a few minutes and then carefully lift it up. You should have the same mix of raw, toasted, and charred fuel you'd get by smothering a tinder bundle in a jar.

Making Fire with Flint and Steel

Now it's time to put your kit to work. Set up the fire lay of your choice and make sure you have ample firewood collected. Make a dry fluffy tinder bundle with available materials, ideally in the shape of a bird's nest, and place a small amount of char material in the center (where the bird eggs would sit). Hold your striker just above the char, usually holding it in your non-dominant hand. Take your sharp stone piece in your dominant hand and strike the stone downward (across the working edge of your striker). If the stone piece is relatively flat, it's best to hold it at a 45-degree angle as this angle helps it to scrape off the steel more effectively. With a loose wrist on your dominant hand, strike the stone against the steel repeatedly, varying your angle and power until you begin throwing sparks. The loose wrist on the hand holding the stone is key. Allow your hand to move as if knocking on a door lightly and quickly. This action should throw sparks downward into your char and you should be able to see the char glow when one catches. In bright daylight, you might not be sure. So, stop periodically and blow gently on the char. If you see it glow in response, you're ready to move to the next step. Once your char has one or more glowing embers in it, fold your bird's nest tinder bundle in half, wrapping fuel all the way around these sparks. Blow steadily on the tinder, focusing the air on the spot that yields the most smoke. Blow as if you were whistling and keep going until the tinder is aflame. Place the burning tinder in your fire lay and watch your fire grow.

Optional Method. There are other positions and motions you can try with flint and steel. I encourage folks to start with the striker held stationary and move the stone downward. This is for practicality and safety, as the technique drives the sparks downward into the waiting char and any stone chips that flake loose are also driven downward (not up into your eyes). If you decide to try something different, another useful technique involves a traditional fuel—actual charred cloth. Little squares of 100 percent cotton or linen cloth can be used for char, and these can also be wrapped around the edge of your flint after charring. Just strike through the brittle cloth and then place the burning char cloth into the tinder.

Troubleshoot Your Problems

One of the unsung skills in fire building is the art of troubleshooting. This is the way to diagnose and correct any issues that are preventing us from finding success. It comes down to basic problem solving, and these are some of the most likely issues you'll face with flint and steel fire lighting.

When the sparks aren't flying:

- Hold your stone at a different angle.
- Try striking with a different edge on the stone.
- Change the pressure of the strike, hitting harder or softer.
- Test a different striking speed or motion.

When good sparks are flying but the char won't catch:

- Move closer to the char, closing the distance the sparks must fly.
- Change your aim, you may be missing the target.
- Switch out your char material, the batch may be damp or bad.

Magnifying Glass

It's hard to imagine how the warm light of a distant sun can get hot enough to cause something to ignite. With the right lens, however, it's far easier than you might think. By concentrating the light through a magnifying lens and providing good tinder at the focal point of the beam—you'll be surprised how quick and effective it can be. The technique is nothing new, either. The use of "burning lenses" is over 2,000 years old, and described by ancient Asian, Greek, and Roman scholars. While rare, clear glass or crystal lenses were known for fire starting, and cauterizing wounds with their intense beam of heat. The first written account of a magnifying lens is actually a humorous line in Aristophanes's play *The Clouds*, written somewhere around 424 BC. At the time, these lenses were sold in apothecary shops and used for various treatments and as an early form of reading glasses. Jump forward to thirteenth-century Italy, and we begin to see the development

The same magnifying glass that young naturalists use to inspect small insects can also be used to get a fire burning.

of actual eyeglasses—which can also light a fire when the prescription is strong enough and the shape rounded.

Today, magnifying lenses are still used for burning—mainly by cruel children who want to burn insects or scorch their name into picnic tables. Often called hand lenses in a laboratory setting, these lenses are typically made from clear glass or plastic, both of which are capable of magnifying sunlight into a white-hot pinpoint of blinding brightness and intense heat.

The Lens. Even though this fire-starting method won't work at night or on a rainy day, there are some unexpected perks to mastering this fire-building method. For one thing, when the matches are long gone and the butane is used up, the magnifying lens will keep on working until you lose it. This reusable tool will last indefinitely and can start an indefinite number of fires as long as the sun keeps shining. The magnifying lens can also light many different types of tinder, even drying them out to make them more suitable to burn.

The Tinder. Now that you know how to make the char cloth used in flint and steel kits, you already know how to make the perfect fuel for a magnifying lens. The same crispy black charred material we'd use for traditional flint and steel fire starting is an excellent choice for optical fire building. The charred material will have a lower ignition temperature than it did when it was raw. Its dark color is also a major asset, since black-colored materials absorb light and heat more readily than light-hued material. As an added benefit, charred materials have a long burn time which can help you to light stubborn or damp tinder bundles. Char cloth is also excellent for catching sparks from ferrocerium rods, not that those tools really need the help under most conditions. And for those situations when you are fresh out of charred material, seek out some fine fibered tinder materials. Collect some dead dry fibrous inner tree bark, the darker colored the better. Pound it with a rock or shred it by hand to separate the plant fibers and expose more surface area. You could also try darker-colored weed tops with fluffy seed down and any other tinder that has proven itself. Form these into a ball and compact them slightly to create a solid surface for the beam of light to hit.

Build a Fire with a Magnifying Lens

With sunny weather overhead and a little bit of practice time under your belt, it's no trouble to focus a blinding pinpoint of sunlight into your tinder bundle. Start by placing a bit of charred tinder into the center of your bundle or setting some of your darker tinder fibers in position. Compact the bundle to create a flat spot in the tinder—this will be your focal point for the light. Move your magnifying lens into position, perpendicular to the sun's light. This bit is important, as you'll need to twist the lens up and down as well as right and left to achieve a circle of light rather than an oval. Once the beam of light has become round, move your lens toward or away from the tinder until you create the smallest focal point of light on the fuel. With the lens position correct, the tinder should begin to smoke immediately. It's often helpful to blow gently on the fuel as the light shines on it. This additional oxygen and air movement can spread the embers that form and cause them to ignite more material. Once the tinder bundle is smoking well, set your lens aside and blow on it until it bursts into flame. Now you have a fire made from light!

Build a Fire with a Bottle of Water

Fire-starting lenses don't all have to be flat magnifying glasses on a stick (that make you look like some kind of investigator). These lenses come in all shapes and sizes. Some of the earliest Greek and Roman models were clear glass globes filled with clear water, and even today, a clear bottle of water can act as a burning lens. Choose a clear glass or plastic bottle with round shoulders as bottles with textured shoulders are actually designed to prevent accidental fires when bottles are discarded as trash. Fill the bottle with perfectly clear water, seal it, and lay it on its side on the ground. Angle it until you see a shimmering focal point of light on the ground and place your char cloth in the light. With the right shape of bottle (and some luck), the tinder will begin to burn.

Use a Fresnel Lens

Even though this item doesn't look like your typical magnifying lens, a flexible plastic Fresnel lens will perform just like a magnifying glass—producing a magnified image of anything behind it and magnifying sunlight. They're also available in many sizes, from large sheets that grab lots of light to small sheets the size of a credit card that are still capable of making fires. The secret of the sheet is that it is comprised of a series of thin concentric ring-shaped lenses. Combined, these thin lenses act like a single thick lens, and they make fire in the same way.

Parabolic Mirror

There's more than one way to concentrate sunlight. In addition to focusing light by passing it through a clear lens, we can also use a curved mirror to redirect sunlight and create an incendiary focal point. The parabolic mirror is a different form of optical fire making, and it originates in the same time-period as the magnifying lens, about 2,000 years ago. The method is steeped in history and is even tied to the ancient origins of the Olympic Games. According to legend, Vestal Virgins would use a curved mirror to light the Olympic torch at the Temple of Hera in Olympia, Greece. The tradition continues today, as actresses playing the role of Greek priestesses still light the Olympic torch with a curved mirror. All this torch wielder needs to do is hold the torch steady at the focal point and wait for the light to heat up the torch head to its ignition point.

Try the Parabolic Mirror for Fire Starting

Step one is to locate a curved mirror of some kind. The shiny curved mirror cup from a large flashlight will work, as will a dismantled round vehicle headlight assembly. These reflecting "cups" can even be made from pieces. For example, you could cover the inside of a bowl with broken glass mirror pieces or mirrored tiles. You may have even seen the "soda can and chocolate" fire method on the internet. This involves polishing the concave bottom of an aluminum beverage can with chocolate as a buffing compound. After hours of polishing (yes, hours), you can create a focal point of heat and light a few inches away from the curved "mirror." It's important to note that deeper mirrors will actually have the focal point inside the concavity and this is what we see with the flashlight mirror. This means that you'll need to remove the flashlight bulb, in addition to removing the mirror from the light. Next, create a small wad of dark tinder and insert it where the flashlight bulb once sat. Tilt the cup right to left and adjust the vertical angle to get a focal point of light inside the cup. When the zenith and azimuth are correct, the tinder should smoke immediately. Blow on the tinder as it smokes, remove it quickly while continuing to blow, and nestle the tinder wad into a larger tinder bundle. Blow that bundle into flame and add it to your ready fire lay. With an understanding of the way to focus sunlight and the right fuels, optical fire starting is one of the easier historic fire-lighting methods, but it does all come down to available light and the right tinder. None of these methods will work from moonlight or starlight. You'll need sunlight. You'll also need a weird mixture of fluffiness and compaction. If the tinder is too dense, it will smolder but have difficulty burning. If the tinder is too fluffy, the scraggly fibers will break up the focal point of light and disrupt the fire attempt. For best results, make your tinder fluffy for flammability, then compact it for a suitable surface to focus your beam of light upon. And as we've discussed, the darker the color—the better it will be at absorbing light and heat.

An old flashlight can provide a parabolic mirror for fire starting.

Matches

Since there are new types of matches on the market every year—especially for survival—you might assume that the match is a relatively new invention. If you paid attention to which chapter you are reading, you've already guessed that the humble match has roots far back in history. That's right, this cheap wad of chemicals on a stick was once dangerous, rare, and costly. Starting at the beginning, Chinese inventors developed simple sulfur matches about 1,500 years ago. These first matches were little pine sticks with flammable sulfur as an added fuel. These weren't intended for day-to-day fire building, that role was served by flint and steel. The match was designated for emergency usage—particularly for lighting lamps quickly. Matches grew in popularity and spread across Asia and Europe. Much later, inventors changed the recipe and began using a much more effective compound. Unfortunately, they didn't realize right away how toxic it was. The famous German alchemist Hennig Brandt discovered white phosphorus in 1669, while looking for a way to turn baser materials into gold.

Fires can be built with cheap kitchen matches or top-quality waterproof survival matches.

Brandt's waxy white phosphorus was remarkable, as it glowed in the dark and was highly combustible. The problem with it wasn't realized until it became heavily used in nineteenth-century match production. It was killing factory workers who were exposed to the material at high levels. Once this toxicity was understood, match factories switched to the safer red phosphorus, which we still use today.

Build a Fire with Matches

Today's most common matches are small wooden sticks and cardboard strips, each with a blend of fire-making chemicals at the tip. This fiery cocktail will ignite when rubbed across an appropriate rough surface. Also known as friction matches, you'll see them sold as safety matches, which only work when struck against a special surface, and strike-anywhere matches, which can be scraped on virtually any rough dry surface. To build a fire with matches, you'll need all the same supplies for any other ignition method. Assemble some good tinder, ample kindling, and a supply of firewood. Choose a fire lay style and get it ready to burn (no gasoline required). Start your fire by striking a match near the base of the fire lay and use your hand to guard the small flame from the wind. Like a candle, the tiny flame from a match can easily be extinguished by a light breeze. Bring the match under the edge of the tinder—low to the ground and on the upwind side of the fire lay. This will allow the wind to push the flames through your fire lay and allow the fire to climb into the fuel. Keep the match in one spot under the tinder for as long as you can stand it. Drop the match into the fire lay once the tinder is engulfed in flame. The average match should burn for ten to fifteen seconds, and this should be long enough to light a well-built fire lay.

Double Your Match Supply

When you're down to the last match in the pack, you'll wish you had been more frugal with these life-saving fire sticks. Well, before things get that bad, there's a trick you can use to extend your supply of fire starters—split each match in half. For paper matches in those little folding books, tear a match from the booklet and carefully start to peel the paper "stick" in half, beginning at the torn end of the match. Try to keep each half of the paper an equal thickness and when you get to the match head, pull it apart quickly to pop the match head in two. These half-thickness matches have a reduced burn time compared to full-sized matches, but they will still ignite and burn and you've effectively doubled your match supply. Strike them by supporting the match head with your finger, dragging them across the striker strip and quickly moving the support finger out of the way so it doesn't get scorched. Now you can get two different fires from each little match.

8 Primitive Fire-Starting Methods

We saved the hardest skills for last. Success with the following friction fire methods will require a lot of practice, the right materials, and a fierce tenacity—so if you think that "rubbing two sticks together" is going to be easy, think again. We'll never know which one of our remote ancestors discovered the secret of fire or what kind of land they occupied. Experts can't even agree on a timetable for fire production. Did we start making our own fires 50,000 years ago? Or was it 500,000 years ago? Our distant past will always be filled with mysteries, but there's one thing we do know—this heritage skill does work. The following methods are all friction fire techniques, and while they are much harder than striking a match, they are still an achievable skill set. With each of these techniques, you'll be grinding wooden pieces together with speed and pressure, rubbing off tiny particles of wood and heating them up. When these little particles clump together favorably and meet or exceed the ignition temperature for that material, they will begin to smolder. With careful handling and good tinder, these smoldering embers can become flames—giving us the gift of fire. As you've seen throughout the fire section, there are different approaches, techniques, and options as you tackle these skills. You'll likely find one of these methods easier than the others, but there isn't a "one size fits all" technique. The conditions you'll face, the materials available, and even your physical prowess will all play a role in your successes and failures. Pay attention to details as you make and use your kits and build up your stamina with these techniques. They'll never be as easy as flicking a lighter, but they do work and they can represent a sustainable backup plan for fire making.

Bow Drills

The bow drill technique is usually the easiest method for beginners to use, thanks to the many "tools" involved in the kit. Rather than

If you need to rub two sticks together to make fire, I hope you have the extra pieces that transform those two sticks into a bow drill kit.

spinning a stick back and forth with your bare hands, you'll use a bow with a string that wraps around the drill. For added stability and downward pressure, you'll use a lubricated socket to hold the top of the drill. With these pieces in place, the drill is pinned between a wooden board and the socket, and as you move the bow back and forth, the string around the drill makes it turn. If you can use this drilling action long enough and hard enough on an effective drill and board, you'll get the ember that you seek. It all starts by building the kit.

Collect the Raw Materials

You'll need eight different things to build a bow drill kit. This may seem like a lot, especially when each piece must fall within certain parameters, but keep working hard and you'll soon have everything you need. The first item is a tool to do the carving and splitting of the wooden pieces, and your handy pocketknife will usually do the job. Second, you'll need tinder to turn ember into flame. Third and fourth, you'll need the friction components. These are the wooden fireboard and drill. You'll also need a flexible bow and strong cord. Finally, you'll require a handhold block and some lubricant for it. Here's where you can find each item.

Pick a Bow

I've told my students for years, "If you have a pile of firewood, you have a pile of bows." Your bow should be a good, strong, flexible stick or branch, roughly the length of your arm and the thickness of your thumb. This stick can be cut or broken from live or dead wood. It can bear a slight curve or be relatively straight. It also doesn't have to be wood. For example, big game rib bones can be flexible and durable bow drill bows.

it's time to apply more lubricant. I usually add a little more to the handhold every time I stop drilling, especially when dealing with wood handhold blocks.

- When your bow is moving back and forth, but the drill isn't turning—it's usually because the cord has started slipping around the drill. Many types of cord will stretch and loosen as you use them. Stop what you're doing and untie one of the knots on the bow. Tie it back in place, a little bit tighter than it was, and try the bow again. If the cord still slips, your cord might be too slick, or you might be pushing downward with too much pressure—locking up the drill between the board and the handhold. Ease up on the downward pressure by 10 to 20 percent and try running the drill again to see if that was the issue.
- You had a good ember, but you lost it! This is a sad occurrence and unfortunately common. When you had a burning ember that was visibly glowing but didn't make a fire, the most likely reason is a bad tinder bundle. When you rush the tinder bundle construction, the result is likely to be coarse and ineffective. Stop what you are doing and rework the tinder. Pound coarse fibers and tear them apart. Add more dry fluffy material to the core of the bundle. Shape it like a bird's nest and try again. Once you have a glowing ember in the nest, blow on it like a whistle and find the spot that makes the most smoke.
- Since water puts out fire, it shouldn't surprise you that moisture can be a serious issue. You'll need to keep your equipment dry if you expect it to work. Moisture in the board and drill are the worst offenders, as they conduct away heat from the friction area and inhibit your chances of forming an ember.

Hand Drills

Take away four of the pieces you'd need for a bow drill kit: the bow, a cord, a handhold block, and lubricant. Then make the drill taller and skinnier. Now spin that drill with your bare hands. This is hand drill fire making. While spinning the drill as quickly as you can, you're also applying downward pressure against the fireboard. This combination of pressure and speed can give us (I didn't say "will give us") the friction and dust to create an ember. How does this stack up against bow drill? A bow drill kit is usually easier for the average person to use, though you'll need twice as many materials to create the kit. The hand drill set only requires four things to make fire—a drill, a fireboard, a tool to carve the board, and some tinder. That makes it quicker to assemble. A good set in the hands of an experienced user can make an

You only need a few items (but a high level of skill) to build a fire with the hand drill method.

ember quickly under favorable weather conditions—but this requires a lot of skill, which only comes through regular practice. Yet with this skill, you only need four objects to make fire. And this technique has been used across the globe and is likely to be the predecessor of bow drill fire making. When you're ready for a tougher challenge, grab the following materials and put your bare hands to work.

Gather Ideal Materials

Since you're lacking the bow and handhold block on this method, you'll want the best materials you can find. Those rotten weed stalks and hardwood fireboards that are within easy reach are not going to do you any favors. Take your time and seek out the best materials you can find for these components. A simple pocket knife or a sharp flake of stone can be enough to cut down the drills and carve the notches in the fireboard. And along with a good tinder bundle, there's a bonus item that is definitely helpful in hand drill fire making: the coal catcher.

Find the Perfect Drill

Tree branches are often the source for bow drill spindles, but these are often too dense and too short for a hand drill. You may get lucky and stumble across dead coppice growth. These are the woody shoots that pop up from the stumps of cut trees, but most of the time, dead dry weed stalks make the best drills. Annual herbaceous plants and some perennial plants will produce flower stalks that grow quickly and straight. Many of these are woody enough once they have died and dried up, and they often have a low ignition temperature. Always wait to collect the flower stalks after the stalk has died or just as it's changing from green to brown. Live stalks will be full of moisture and useless until they dry out. The average drill stalk is between 20 and 30 inches in length, and the straighter the better. The thickest part should be about ½ inch in diameter. Great species choices include yucca, velvet leaf, lambs quarters, horseweed, mullein, dog fennel, and goldenrod. If you intend to use the stalks immediately, choose the driest ones available. You may also want to cut off the bottom 6 to 12 inches of the stalk, as this will be the end you'll spin against the fireboard, and it will naturally be damp as it's closer to the ground. Make sure that your stalks are not too old or rotten. You'll want them dead but still strong. If you plan to use the stalks later, it's fine if they are wet or even slightly green. These can be dried out for a few days or weeks and used when ready.

Carve a Fireboard

The hand drill fireboard is very similar to the bow drill fireboard, though the dimensions are scaled down quite a bit. These are best used as smaller and thinner boards, and ideally, they are the same thickness as your drill diameter. The soft wood species mentioned for bow drill boards will usually work well for a hand drill board. Willow is one of my favorites for this, but you should try different local species to see which ones are the best in your area. This board will require a hole and notch just like a bow drill board, just scaled down in size to better match the drill diameter.

Find a Coal Catcher

We've talked about the four items you need for a hand drill fire: drill, board, tinder, and tool. This will get you a fire, but life will be much easier with an extra item—a "coal catcher." We mentioned something like this in the bow drill section, as a dead leaf that can go under your fireboard notch. This extra piece is even more important with a hand drill kit, as the coals are smaller and more fragile. Your coal catcher can be any thin flat material that will fit well under your fireboard to collect dust. It's used to transfer your ember into the tinder without disturbing it. A thick dead dry leaf will work just fine, and I commonly use thin strips of dead inner tree bark taken from the tinder pile. For the most durable coal catcher, use a sharp knife to slice a flat wide wood shaving from the fireboard or another piece of wood. Place this piece under the fireboard notch before you start your fire-making attempt, and it will be in place to help you transport the ember (hopefully).

Build the Hand Drill Kit

Just like the bow drill, kit craftsmanship is one of the keys to your success. Even though there are fewer pieces to make, don't just throw a kit together. Use your knife to cut out the straightest section of each weed stalk, then take a rough stone or some sandpaper to sand off all the rough places on the stalk. You don't want it to be polished or slick, this will hamper your ability to grip the stalk. Just make sure there aren't any spots that feel sharp or rough, as these will tear up the skin on your palms. With the drill done, prepare the piece that will become the hand drill fireboard. If you have a thick stick or branch, try splitting it lengthwise with a knife. Choose the best looking half and improve it. Carve the split side to make it flatter. This will eliminate some of the wobble in the board. You can also carve the top of the board to be flatter. Your fireboard doesn't have to look like a perfect plank of lumber. It just needs to be stable when you place your foot on it. Use your tool to drill a pilot hole in the top of the board. Make this on one end, placed close to the edge. Grab your weed stalk drill and spin it in the pilot hole to mate the two surfaces. Spin enough that you begin to burn down into the board. The last step in board construction is carving the notch. This should be cut into the side of the board, and it should be a 45-degree notch like your bow drill board (just smaller proportions). This notch should run from the edge of the board to the center of the circle. Now you're ready to try the hand drill set.

Make Your First Hand Drill Fire

Spinning a weed stalk between your hands isn't a very complex action. Even a child can do it. The complex part comes when you must spin the drill and maintain downward pressure at the same time. Starting near the top of the stalk, begin spinning the stalk with slow and even strokes, using as much of each hand as is comfortable (don't just spin with your palms and ignore your fingers). Once you are spinning comfortably, increase your speed, push your palms tighter together, and start pushing downward. This downward pressure is necessary for friction, but unfortunately, it also causes your hands to slide down the stalk. Once you near the bottom of the stalk, you won't be moving

With the right materials and after a lot of practice (and blisters), the hand drill ember can be brought to life.

effectively anymore. You'll have to briefly stop spinning and move back to the top of the drill. Keep this up until you are making ample smoke and your notch is overflowing with dust. Once you have enough dust, increase your speed spinning the stalk to reach the ignition temperature of the dust. If the kit is good enough (and you are too), the dust will turn into an ember. If the smoke stops a few seconds after you stop drilling, then you've only produced dust—not an ember. Just leave the dust in the notch, catch your breath and try again.

Tricks That Help

This friction fire method can be tricky enough on a good day, even if the equipment is perfect and you have no extra problems. For this reason, it's smart to stack the deck in your favor, learning to identify problems and taking advantage of any tricks that eliminate those problems.

Keep the Kit Dry

Moisture is a common culprit in hand drill difficulties. Store your drills and fireboards in a dry place or dry them out prior to use. For example, you may be able to get better results after drying your kit in the sun for a few hours. Even with great kit components and skillful hand drill technique, dampness can keep you from making an ember.

Increase Your Traction

This seems contradictory to the last tip, but the focused placement of moisture or stickiness can be very helpful. Instead of spinning a dry weed stalk drill, add something that increases your traction on the stalk. Most people will spit on their hands prior to spinning the stalk. This moisture improves your grip slightly. Just don't let a gob of spittle run down the drill and into the fire hole. It's just a little spit on your hands, then rub them together, then start drilling. Alternately, you can rub a piece of hard dry pine sap on the weed stalk. This will make the surface slightly sticky and improve your grip.

Match Your Pieces

You may be able to create embers from a wide range of materials and kit combinations, but it's very helpful to try matching your kit components based on similar density and wood quality. When a drill is too dense for its board, the drill will cut through the board too quickly. When a fireboard is too dense, the dust production may not be good enough. You'll have the best results with matching pieces.

Practice Regularly

There's no substitute for regular training and practice. Without this practice, many different skills can grow "rusty," especially challenging skills like hand drilling. Keep a hand drill set in a handy place, like your coffee table, and make a little practice time each day. If this practice makes too much smoke, upgrade your training set to a hardwood drill and board. Once that starts making smoke, try adding lubricant to the set. When your technique is good enough to burn off the lube and smoke up the hardwood set, your hand drill skills should yield fires on a regular basis. Just a little practice will build your strength, increase your stamina, and toughen up those callouses—making you a much more effective fire builder.

Mix It Up

The hand drill doesn't exist in a bubble, and there's nothing in the rule book that says you can't combine some bow drill technology with the hand drill technique. The easiest way to hybridize the two methods is with a buddy. You may not be able to get a hand drill ember by yourself, but the help of a second person may yield a success. The first person will run the hand drill as normal. The second person will take a well-lubricated bow drill handhold block and hold it on top of the drill. As one person spins the hand drill, the other person applies downward pressure on the handhold. Communicate with each other to establish the right amount of downward pressure. If there's not enough pressure, you won't get an ember. If the helper pushes downward too hard, it will cause the drill to lock up. Talk it through and find the right pressure.

Build Up the Ember

Due to the inconsistent pressures of the hand drill, these embers are very different from bow drill embers. Not only are they smaller, but they are also loose and often consist of multiple ember "lumps." These fragile embers can be enhanced by adding a small amount of powdery fuel into them. This fuel could be the dust from previous fire attempts that didn't form an ember. The dust could also be fine sawdust scraped from flammable fungus species, such as polypore shelf fungi and chaga. The fluffy seed down from cattail plants and other fine "parachute" seed material will work well. Simply sprinkle a little bit of this material on top of a struggling hand drill ember and allow it to sit for a few seconds. This feeds the ember and once the new material is smoldering, move it into your tinder.

Add Some Training Wheels

It's not easy for beginners to press their hands together hard enough to transfer the pressure downward on the drill. Without this downward pressure, you'll never get the necessary friction and heat to create an ember. Luckily, there's a simple trick that can help with downward pressure. By tying a string over the top of the drill and adding a loop to each end, the user can place their thumbs in the loops and get an assist with downward pressure. These training wheels aren't a perfect solution, as they tend to reinforce poor hand drill technique. However, they can make the difference between success and failure, and it's a technique worth trying out especially when you're really close to getting an ember, but it just won't happen on its own.

Fire Saw

Anyone who works with bamboo is already familiar with the interesting combination of flexibility, strength, and lightness of this special material. So, it shouldn't come as a surprise to crafters that this woody substance can also make a very unusual friction fire method. The bamboo fire saw is ancient, and it has been commonly used in many parts of Asia as well as many Pacific islands. In keeping with its unique manner, the bamboo saw is one of the few friction fire-starting methods that can be done with only one material. That's right, you only need

When bamboo is available, fire builders can try a unique method, the bamboo fire saw.

bamboo! Bamboo can even produce the tinder and kindling to start the fire. As an added bonus, it even has a low ignition temperature. The method works by sawing one piece of bamboo against another one until one piece cuts a significant gap through the other. If all goes to plan, charred bamboo dust flows into the tinder and an ember is born.

Build the Fire Saw Kit

As with everything worth doing, you'll need to put in some hard work, show your talent, and have the right materials in order to have success with the bamboo fire saw. But when everything goes right, just a little bit of bamboo dust can form a glowing ember that is capable of lighting a mighty fire. Start by locating some dry bamboo around 3 inches in diameter (most of the larger species will work). Pick out a nice dead, ideally yellow-colored, section of bamboo. If all you have are short sections, around one foot long, split a piece in half and plan to do the "short" piece method. If longer sections are available, choose one that is about 3 to 4 feet long.

The "Long" Method

With a hand saw or a sharp broken edge of bamboo, saw out a "half" section of bamboo between two nodes—these are the solid joints—and near to one end of the piece of bamboo. This "half-round" piece will become the "tray" component and the piece it came from will give you your choice of two saw edges. The tray is the component that moves back and forth. The tray is also the part that holds the tinder and receives the dust. To make things easier, I use the tip of my knife as a drill to ream a small hole through the tray where I plan to do the sawing. This gives me a clear path for the dust to travel, and I don't have to wait for the saw to cut a gap completely on its own. In addition to the tray, you'll need tinder and an additional piece to hold the tinder in place. Often referred to as the "bridge" stick, this can be a twig or a slender strip of bamboo. And if you want to make it interesting, you can even make your tinder from the bamboo for an "all bamboo" fire. Take a sharp metal blade or stone scraper and scrape it briskly against the outside of a bamboo piece. For a knife, hold the edge around 90 degrees to the bamboo surface and scrape hard. If the angle is right, thin curls of bamboo will come off. These curly shavings will fall into a pile and after several minutes of brisk scraping, you'll have enough tinder to build a fire. Reserve some for the fire saw tray and keep a larger pile for a tinder bundle to light your fire lay.

Try the "Long" Saw Technique

With a tinder pile made, the tray pre-drilled with a pilot hole, and a bridge stick chosen, it's time to get the kit ready for use.

Take the long piece of bamboo and use a knife or scraper to carve or scrape a slightly sharp edge on each of the exposed edges of bamboo where the tray came from. This will help your chosen edge cut into the tray. I usually sharpen them both, though you'll only use one at a time. Then I'll prepare the tray. Make two small compact wads of tinder and place them in your tray, one on each side of the pilot hole. Rest the bridge over the tinder and hold the ends of the bridge stick with your thumbs. This bridge and tinder combination is vital, as it gives your ember a place to form and keeps the dust from being lost as you saw back and forth. Once these things are in place, pin the long piece of bamboo between your hip and the ground. It's nice to have some padding, like a wad of cloth or some other padding, between the bamboo and your hip bone. Squat a bit and bring one leg forward to support the underside of the bamboo against your thigh. Start sliding the tray back and forth against one of the sharp edges of the long bamboo piece. Saw directly over the pilot hole, so that the slot is abraded away in the correct spot and so that your dust flows through the pilot hole. When you can tell that a groove has formed and you are sawing in the right spot, increase the saw speed and pressure. The kit should begin smoking and dust should be flowing into the tray. Increase to your maximum speed and pressure for about thirty more seconds and stop. Blow into the tinder in your tray, and if there is an ember inside, the smoke will increase rather than being blown away and dissipating. If the smoke did not continue, catch your breath and try again. You should be able to try twice on each hole through the tray without cutting the tray so deeply that you risk snapping it in two. If you do have an ember, gently remove the bridge stick, then move the tinder and ember from the tray to larger tinder bundle. Blow the tinder into flame.

Use the "Short" Method

When shorter bamboo sections are your only choice, try the method that reverses the position of the saw and tray components. By placing the tray on the ground with abundant tinder underneath, you can saw back and forth on top of it with a sharp-edged piece of bamboo. You can begin with a pilot hole through the tray or allow the saw to cut all the way through. This sawing action will cut through the tray and drop hot dust down into the tinder, hopefully creating an ember under the tray. This method takes a bit more control than the "long" method, but it takes advantage of smaller bamboo pieces and that's all you may have to use.

Make Bamboo Kindling

Bamboo isn't just a good material for friction components and tinder. You can also create a very nice kindling material from it. Create bright burning kindling by splitting down

(continued next page)

woody bamboo segments with a sharp knife. This can be done by hand or by striking the spine of the knife with a baton to drive it through the bamboo sections. Bamboo splits easily with the grain (lengthwise with the stalks). Break down these split pieces into little strips that are matchstick diameter for ideal kindling.

Troubleshoot Your Fire Saw Kit

To most people, the fire saw technique is comparable in difficulty and reliability to the bow drill method. And like most other friction fire methods, there are plenty of pieces that can fail and hampering issues to face. Here are some tricks that can help you succeed in your quest for friction fire.

Be Choosey with Materials

Since material selection plays such a huge role in every friction fire method, you'll want to pick the best bamboo pieces that are available. These should be dead and dry, but not rotten. Color is a great indicator for many bamboo species. Look for dull, yellow-colored pieces or weathered grey ones. Skip the green bamboo. It contains too much moisture.

Keep the Saw Sharp

How good is a dull saw? Whether cutting for wood or using the saw technique with woody materials to make the fire, it's helpful to use a knife or other cutting tool to create a sharper cutting edge on the saw piece. A sharper edge generates more pressure, and it also cuts into the tray more effectively.

Easy Does It

You'll want to start off slowly and make sure that the saw edge and the hole in the tray are aligned together. If this is a regular problem for you, carve a slight groove across the hole on the outside of the tray. The groove will act as a guide for the saw edge and keep things in position without slipping off track.

Not Too Loose

That dust is critical and you don't want to lose it or the ember that it can form. Keep your dust in place and protect that ember by packing your tinder tight as it sits around the hole in the tray. Due to the fluffy nature of tinder, you don't have to worry about packing it too tight. The dust will find its way through the airy material.

Breathe Deeply, Breathe Often

Like the brutal fire plow and other physically demanding friction fire methods, you have to breathe deeply to keep up your cardio. Many people tend to hold their breath when performing these actions, but without deep breathing, you'll run out of energy long before you ever make an ember. If you find yourself forgetting to breathe deeply, then bark, chant, yell, swear, grunt, or make any other noise to keep that air moving in and out of your lungs. You need oxygen just as much as that fire does.

Fire Plow

This brutal friction fire-making method may just be the oldest method in the bunch, and it's certainly the most demanding. The fire plow is as raw as things can get. You are grinding one piece of wood against another until you wear down a small trench in the bigger piece. Then you'll continue to grind away until you fill the groove with enough dust and reach a high enough temperature to create an ember. It's full-contact fire making and a serious cardio workout. The advantages of this method are few. However, it can be done without any tools, and you only need two pieces of wood and some tinder to turn a smoking ember into flame. But this is the hardest way I know to coax an ember into life, so you'd better be talented and tenacious.

This brutal and simplistic method is the hardest way to create friction fire, but it does occasionally work.

Be Choosey with Your Materials

Two pieces of wood and some tinder—these are the only physical objects you'll need to get fire with the fire plow. However, you shouldn't allow this simplicity to fool you into the assumption that this is going to be easy. On the contrary, you'll have to put the work in somewhere. It may take a long time and many pieces to make a bow drill kit, but this effort comes back to you with an easier fire-making attempt. All those "tools" you made will make the friction process easier. Similarly, when a fire kit is easy to throw together, you're going to pay for it on the back end—the kit will generally be harder to use. Keep that in mind as you collect the materials for the fire plow and be choosey when it comes to species and conditions. Look for a softwood plow stick that is around two feet in length. It should be roughly the thickness of your thumb. This is the moving component of your kit. For this piece, I like to use thick dry yucca flower stalks, the fatter the better. This stick could also be made from basswood, pawpaw, or willow branch. Skip the hardwood species as a plow stick. They will make smoke and cut a groove into a softwood log, but the ignition temperature of their dust will likely be too high for good results.

Your second component will be a softwood log or large wooden plank. This is the component that you'll grind the plow stick across and the piece which will develop a groove. This piece should be dead dry wood, without any significant level of rot or decay. Rotten wood has usually lost too much fuel value to be an effective friction fire kit component. Try to find a piece that has a flat bottom or a fork on one end. These features will brace the piece and keep it steady while you plow against it. Good species for this are basswood, white cedar, aspen, willow, and other soft wood logs. These would ideally be cut into half-round sections and placed with the flat side on the ground to avoid wobbling or rolling.

It's All About the Technique

When I set out to attempt the fire plow, I will usually try to pin down my plow surface to the ground for stability. I like to butt it up against a solid object, like a tree trunk or a large rock. If that's not convenient, I'll drive a large stake into the ground and butt the plow surface up against that. In damp conditions with wet ground, I also like to build a barrier under the plow surface to keep the ground moisture from wicking up into the wooden piece. This could be a pile of dead dry leaves, some bark slabs, or even thin flat stone slabs. Once you are ready to "plow," you'll have three different fire-making techniques you can try. The method I use the most involves grinding the plow stick back and forth, trying to stop in exactly the same spot at the end of each stroke. If you can do this repeatedly, you'll create a groove in the plow surface and build up dust in that groove on top of a little "step" at the end of the groove. A different and slightly less successful approach is to plow right off the end of the plow surface with each stroke. This pushes all your hot dust off the end of the plow surface so that it forms a small pile at the end of the plow surface. A third approach that works for some people although it is very unpredictable is to run the plow stick in the groove as hard and fast as you can. Don't worry about pushing dust into a pile inside your groove or pushing it off the end of the plow surface. You'll place fluffy tinder like cattail down along both sides of the plow surface and plow like a maniac. With the right materials and effort, little embers will be kicked out of the groove and fall into the tinder. The first method mentioned is my best recommendation for novice fire makers. To use this method, brace the far end of your plow surface against the support as mentioned earlier and then place one or both of your knees at the other end of the plow surface. This pins the surface down and puts you right in position to work. Alternately, you could have a friend sit or stand on the plow surface or choose a dry log that is heavy enough to stay put on its own. Begin working the plow stick back and forth on top of the plow surface. This will abrade away the desired groove and it will begin to produce dust and heat. This initial groove should be one foot long or a little shorter. Breathe deeply as you move the plow stick and speed up when you have created a groove that the plow stick can follow. You should produce smoke once you begin to form the groove, and the wood will darken once you start producing good dust. For best results, try to stop the plow stick at the end of each stroke in the exact same spot. This will form a small shelf inside the groove, and it will make it easier to stop in the same place on each subsequent stroke. Keep working hard, breathing deeply and producing dust. Once you see a dust pile at the end of the groove on top of your shelf, use the plow stick even faster and harder. This final burst of speed might just create the ember that you've worked so hard to get. If there's a reddish glow in the dust pile, you've won! If the pile stops smoking and there is no glow, you lost. If the dust doesn't ignite, catch your breath and try again. You can also make a team attempt by asking another person to jump in there and keep plowing while the pieces are hot. This is how we have the best luck in my survival camp, swapping out people quickly and leaving the dust in the groove. Good luck. This is the toughest friction fire method.

Troubleshoot the Fire Plow

Just because it's a barbaric way to make fire doesn't mean that it's an impossible way to do it. There are some ways to improve the set and your technique. Try these troubleshooting tips if you need a helping hand.

Reduce Some Surface Area

A fat plow stick will often feel like it's hanging up in the log groove. You'll know it for certain when your output of smoke and dust drop off quickly. The solution is simple: carve a slice away from each side of the tip on the plow stick. This reduces the wasted side friction in the groove and it adds to the pressure you are applying downward.

Flip the Point

By abrading away the plow stick on one side, your plow stick will naturally form a beveled point that spreads out your applied pressure over a wide area. This does nothing to help your effort. Bring your pressure back to maximum by flipping the plow stick over. This puts the sharper point in contact with the log, ramping up your pressure and generating maximum heat.

Keep Plowing

If you want the fire badly enough, you'll keep plowing as long as you can. For morale and also to force the user to breathe deeply, certain cultures have been known to chant or shout while grinding away on the fire plow. This makes for a very entertaining show, but more importantly, it forces you to breathe harder and deeper. Without deep breathing, your cardio output will drop off quickly and your performance will soon take a nosedive. If you feel a little self-conscious by improvising a savage tribal chant, then breathe out deeply at the end of each stroke. This will force you to breathe deeply and in a regular pattern, and that may make all the difference.

9
Fire Maintenance and Safety

With more than a dozen fire-making techniques at your disposal now, we finish the fire section with the subjects that impact them all—the maintenance of a fire and the safe use of fire. As you have learned, the thing we call fire is much more than just a marshmallow roasting heat resource or some friendly supply of warmth for campers in the wild. It is part of the natural cycle in many environments. For untold ages of the earth, naturally occurring wildfires have been a tool for renewal in ecosystems around the planet. As a purging force of nature, wildfires transform dead undergrowth into nourishing ashes, rich in the minerals that plants need for healthy growth. These fires may seem catastrophic at the time, but they open up space for new growth and regenerate the land. When these fires happen naturally and run their course in small areas, they restore balance. Today, we have a very different relationship to these natural cycles. As increasing numbers of humans live and travel through fire prone areas, we tend to stop most fires before they do their normal work—clearing away dead brush and flammable materials. Unchecked, this undergrowth can reach dangerous levels, creating wildfires that even man cannot control. It is because of these conditions that we cannot afford to be careless with fire. In the wrong place and time, a fire may escape your care and consume wilderness areas, homes, and lives. In this final chapter, we'll look at some tricks for fire maintenance, how to extinguish a fire effectively, and what to do if a fire turns against you. Remember, fire is more than a tool for survival—when it gets out of control, it can be the threat that you are trying to survive.

Fire Maintenance

You've learned the fuels that fire requires. And you've learned the ignition methods, of both yesteryear and today. Now we'll work on the maintenance of your campfire. Fire is an unrestricted chain reaction, meaning that it can go on indefinitely. As long as the fuel, heat, and oxygen continue to be provided, the fire will continue to burn. Since the air is generally free for the taking, this leaves you to manage the heat and fuel. Luckily for us, the heat will maintain itself if the fuel keeps flowing, so the only thing we really have to worry about is feeding our "pet" fire. This can be done with many different fuels. If you only have small materials, like twigs and sticks, you'll have to feed your fire very frequently. When you have larger pieces of slow burning wood, you may only have to feed it once an hour or less. Your goal as a fire manager is to feed the fire an appropriate amount of "food." Feed it too much and the fire will grow larger than necessary. Fail to feed it enough and your fire can literally starve to death. Feed the fire the right amount and it can burn indefinitely. Just remember to never light a fire too big to put out with the methods you have readily available.

Keep a Fire Going All Night

The trick of "banking" up a fire is an ancient one, but it also seems to have fallen into the category of legend among modern outdoor enthusiasts. Many people have heard of the technique, but few have ever tried it. The skill is very easy, and it can keep a few coals alive through most of the night (six to eight hours, if everything goes right). All you have to do is build up a thick bed of embers, ideally from slow burning hardwood logs. Then cover the bed of embers completely with several inches of dry dirt, sand, or ashes. This "bank" of dirt will smother the fire and cause it to burn very slowly, usually without putting the fire out completely. You can extend the life of the embers by adding some green firewood or any other slow-burning fuel before you bury the embers. You can also protect the "bank" from rain by placing a large thin flat rock over the pile, angled slightly to create a roof. In the morning, dig through the pile and blow on it. Any remaining embers will glow in response to the air flow. Place one of these in tinder and bring your fire back to life.

How to Extinguish a Fire

When it's time to put your fire out completely, your best solution is to drown the fire with a generous amount of water. If you have time, let the fire burn down until it is mostly ashes. Use a sturdy stick to spread out the remaining wood, ash, and charcoal within the fire pit as burning materials will extinguish better when they are not touching. Drown these hot materials with plenty of water. It doesn't need to be clean drinking water, just dip some raw water from a local source. Using your stick again, stir the water, ashes, and embers to mix them thoroughly. In areas with soil that is full of dry organic material, it's also smart to use your stick to poke holes into the ground underneath the fire to allow the water to penetrate deeply. Check the surrounding rocks and area for live embers, and pour more water on them, if necessary. If water is absent in your location or too scarce to waste, you can allow the fire to burn out completely—until the ashes are cool and dead. You could also bury the fire with dirt, though this can "bank" the fire and keep the embers alive for hours. In any event, never leave your camp until your campfire is out completely.

Wildfire Prevention

A fire that has escaped human control can be a powerful and destructive force of nature. As we discussed in Chapter Five, you'll want to choose a safe fire location before you even think about striking the first match. In addition to keeping your fire away from your shelter, dead stumps, dry brush, and other fire risks, it's also helpful to choose a spot that has been used for fire before. Existing fire rings and hearths are often the safest spots to start your fire, since they offer a protective structure and it's likely that most of the surrounding flammable materials have already burned. When your camp site lacks an existing ring or hearth, set one up yourself. These aren't complicated to build from scratch, even when tools are lacking. Choose a place that is at least fifteen feet (five meters) from brush, dry grass, dead ground cover, fallen foliage, and other flammable materials. Watch out for dead foliage overhead, too. You'll want to clear away a ten-foot (three-meter) circle where nothing can burn, sweeping or raking away sticks, leaves, and all other flammable materials. Next, dig a shallow pit in the ground. It only needs to be one foot (thirty cm) deep, or even a little less. Encircle the pit with the soil you excavated or a ring of rocks. If you choose rocks, just make sure you collect them from a dry location. Rocks that are picked out of waterways are often waterlogged. These can explode violently when the water turns to steam inside the rock, as it can do next to a hot fire. Keep your fire inside this pit and be prepared to put the fire out if the wind gets high enough to start blowing sparks and embers outside of your cleared area. You'll also want to think twice before you build a fire in certain conditions, with or without a pit. Wildfires can occur in a wide range of habitats and conditions. Certain ones are obvious, like fields full of dead grass and dry summer pine forests. Others are not as expected, but still a threat such as a swampy area during a bad "dry season" or a drought. Any place with abundant dead vegetation could be a potential wildfire location, and combinations of dry weather and wind will make them even worse.

What to Do in a Wildfire

You've tried your best to create a safe fire area and watched over your fire, but the worst has happened. It has escaped your control. Since we are killed by fire just as easily as animals, it's important to know what to do and where to go in this frightening scenario.

One of the most useful techniques is to submerge yourself in a nearby river, lake, or some other body of water. Remove a piece of clothing and get it wet. Place the wet cloth over your face, and lie back in the water, exposing as little skin as possible. The wet cloth will act like a heat shield—and equally important—it will filter out some of the smoke in the air. When water isn't available as a haven, try to find some other protection from the fire. If you're near a road, lie face down along the road in a ditch or depression, or crawl under the road if you can squeeze into a culvert or drainpipe. You could also look for natural gaps in the fuel for the wildfire, which could mean breaks in the trees, grass, brush, or other vegetation. When there's a gap in the fuel, there will be gap in the fire. Similarly, when you are caught out in the open, you may be able to move into an area that has already been burnt in a previous wildfire. It's counterintuitive and a risky move to try outmaneuvering a fire, but these areas may stall the fire since some of the fuel was burnt in a previous fire. So, what's the worst place to get caught near a wildfire? In most conditions, the worst place to be is uphill from the fire and downwind from the flames. The wind is a major player in the movement of the fire, and by paying attention to the wind direction, the breeze can literally point you in the right direction. When the wind is blowing from your position toward the fire, then you should run into the wind. But if the wind is behind the fire, blowing toward you, run on a course that puts you perpendicular to the wind, and move fast. That fire will be coming at you quickly. But as you move in relation to the wind, make sure to avoid canyons and other natural chimneys. The natural air flow patterns of these places could suck in a fire like a chimney for a fireplace and the landforms could trap you. And when you can't get out of the fire's path, use anything you can find that provides a shield against the heat. Get into a low spot, cover your face with wet cloth, and cover your body with sand, soil, mud, or anything else non-flammable that can block the heat.

Closing

With these secrets of water and fire, you should now be better prepared for all kinds of emergencies—both in the wilderness and even in the wake of a disaster. I've provided you with the information, skills, tips, and tricks to become a model survivalist (at least in the realms of water procurement and fire building). My work is done, but yours is only beginning. Now it's time for you to practice these skills and become a master in your own right. And now I'll give you a final warning.

A book is a dangerous thing in some regards. In sharing one's experiences, the author can convey a lot of information. This can save the reader a lot of time and trouble, shortening the learning curve, and improving someone's skills significantly. But at the end of the day, these shared stories and experiences are someone else's information. It's not really your own experience, not until you get out there and get your hands dirty. Gaining your own experience by practicing survival skills is the best way to learn and remember new information. So, we encourage you to do more than just read this book. We encourage you to try these skills in a safe and practical setting. Learn to build a fire with different methods. Learn to harvest water from different places. These are the skills of our ancestors, and they are part of our heritage, but you can't really own these skills until you've done them yourself. It's better to be over-prepared and succeed, than to be overconfident and fail.

Best wishes and good luck!
Tim MacWelch

Index

Also Available

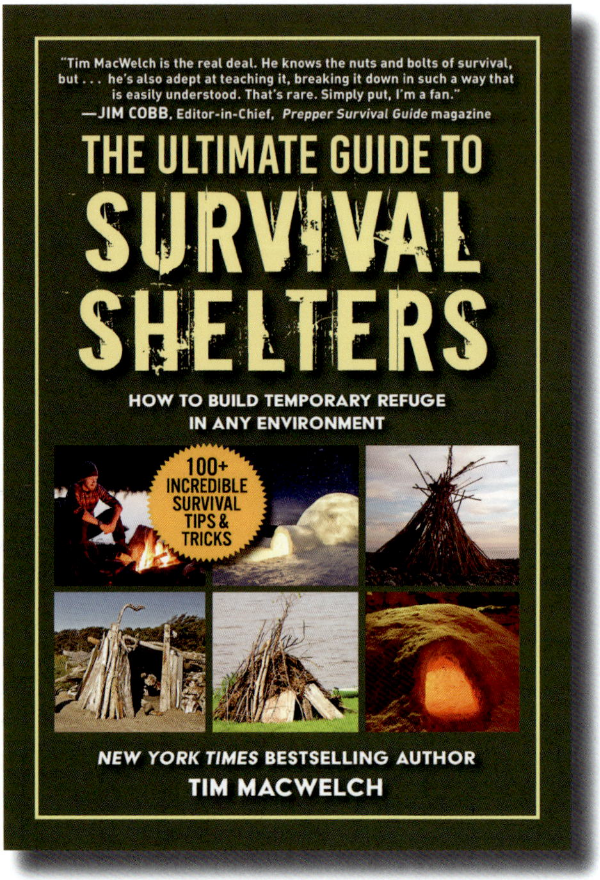

New York Times bestselling author and survival school founder, Tim MacWelch shows us why shelter is our top survival priority in most emergency situations, and how we can provide ourselves with this lifesaving resource. In *The Ultimate Guide to Survival Shelters*, MacWelch details our risks for exposure (from both the heat and cold) and guides readers through the myriad of options for providing this necessary resource. Learn how to find, enhance, and build shelters in a wide range of environments and survival situations, and learn how to get by with less than you might have imagined. *The Ultimate Guide to Survival Shelters* provides the tools to become a problem-solver and think outside the box in any situation.

Print ISBN: 978-1-5107-5556-7 | Ebook ISBN: 978-1-5107-5847-6